EGYPTIAN MYTHOLOGY

A Timeless Collection of Egyptian Myths and Legends

Adrian Danvers

CONTENTS

Copyrights	IV
Free Bonus	1
Introduction	2
Chapter 1: The Egyptian Pantheon	4
Chapter 2: Other Characters of Egyptian Mythology	41
Chapter 3: Creation Myths	55
Chapter 4: Life in Ancient Egypt	62
Chapter 5: Isis and Osiris	67
Chapter 6: The Story of Rhodopis	74
Chapter 7: The Tale of Two Brothers	76
Chapter 8: The Journey of Ra	79
Chapter 9: The Book of Thoth	82
Chapter 10: Isis and the Seven Scorpions	87
Chapter 11: The Destruction of Mankind	90
Chapter 12: Cats and Bastet	94
Chapter 13: The Prince and the Sphinx	96
Conclusion	98
More Books By Adrian Danvers	100

Copyright © 2024 by Dreamtime Books LLC

All rights reserved.

No portion of this book may be reproduced in any form without written permission from the publisher or author, except as permitted by U.S. copyright law.

This publication is designed to provide accurate and authoritative information in regard to the subject matter covered. It is sold with the understanding that neither the author nor the publisher is engaged in rendering legal, investment, accounting or other professional services. While the publisher and author have used their best efforts in preparing this book, they make no representations or warranties with respect to the accuracy or completeness of the contents of this book and specifically disclaim any implied warranties of merchantability or fitness for a particular purpose. No warranty may be created or extended by sales representatives or written sales materials. The advice and strategies contained herein may not be suitable for your situation. You should consult with a professional when appropriate. Neither the publisher nor the author shall be liable for any loss of profit or any other commercial damages, including but not limited to special, incidental, consequential, personal, or other damages.

FREE BONUS

Thanks for taking the time to pick up this book all about Egyptian Mythology!

As a thank you, I've put together a book detailing the Creation Myths from 20 different ancient cultures, and it's yours for free! These creation myths laid the foundation for how the people viewed and understood the world around them.

All you need to do, is head to www.adriandanvers.com to claim your free copy. Alternatively, you can scan the QR code below.

Thanks again, I hope you enjoy it!

INTRODUCTION

Embarking on a journey through the sands of time, "Egyptian Mythology: A Timeless Collection of Egyptian Myths and Legends" unveils the rich tapestry of stories that have shaped one of the world's oldest civilizations. This book is an invitation to explore the enigmatic world of Egyptian gods, mythical beings, creation myths, and the daily lives of its people, woven through the vibrant legacy of ancient Egypt.

In the opening chapter, we delve into the celestial realm of the Egyptian pantheon, introducing the reader to the gods and goddesses who played pivotal roles in the lives and afterlives of the ancient Egyptians. From the sun god Ra, embodying life and creation, to the complex and multifaceted Isis, goddess of magic and motherhood, each deity's story is a thread in the intricate fabric of Egyptian cosmology.

Chapter two broadens our exploration to include the mortals, demi-gods, and mythical creatures that populate Egyptian myths, such as the visionary architect Imhotep, the sacred Apis Bull, the devourer of the unworthy, Ammit, and the phoenix-like Bennu bird, symbolizing rebirth. These characters enrich the myths with their tales of ingenuity, devotion, and transformation.

The narrative deepens in the third chapter with a dive into the creation myths that form the foundation of Egyptian cosmology. From the primordial chaos of the Hermopolis myth to the sun god's emergence in Heliopolis, the artisan god Ptah's vision in Memphis, and the hidden aspects of Amun in Thebes, these stories offer diverse perspectives on the universe's origins and the gods' manifestation.

Chapter four transitions from the celestial to the terrestrial, painting a vivid picture of daily life in ancient Egypt. It explores how the people lived, worked, and worshipped, revealing how deeply their lives were intertwined with the divine and the myths that influenced their rituals, art, and society.

The heart of the book recounts the legendary myths that have endured through millennia, such as the tragic and triumphant tale of Isis and Osiris, the Cinderella-like story of Rhodophis, the fraternal saga of The Tale of Two Brothers, and the celestial journey of Ra across the sky. These stories, among others, highlight the themes of love, betrayal, justice, and redemption that resonate with the human experience.

"Egyptian Mythology: A Timeless Collection of Egyptian Myths and Legends" is not just a book; it's a portal to a world where gods walk among men, where mythical creatures soar through the skies, and where the mighty Nile flows through the heart of a civilization that has captivated the human imagination for centuries. Join us on this journey through the myths and legends that continue to enchant and inspire.

CHAPTER 1: THE EGYPTIAN PANTHEON

The Egyptian pantheon is vast and complex, with numerous gods and goddesses who were worshipped throughout different time periods and locations in ancient Egypt. It is nearly impossible to compile a comprehensive list of every single deity, as there are hundreds of them, and some are only mentioned in passing or are known from a single artifact. However, in this chapter we will explore an extensive list of some of the most important and widely recognized gods and goddesses in the ancient Egyptian pantheon. However, it is important to note that there were many more minor deities and regional gods worshipped throughout ancient Egypt, and their importance could vary greatly over time and from place to place.

Firstly, however, it's important to make note of the different time periods that Ancient Egyptian history is divided into, as some Gods and Goddesses were more prominent and revered during different periods in the country's long history.

Egypt's history is typically divided into different periods, with each period marked by distinct political, social, and cultural characteristics. These periods include:

1. **Early Dynastic Period (c. 3100-2686 BCE):** Also known as the Archaic Period, this era saw the unification of Upper and Lower Egypt under a single ruler, King Narmer. The first two dynasties of pharaohs ruled during this time, establishing the foundations of the Egyptian

state.

2. **Old Kingdom (c. 2686-2181 BCE):** This period, which encompasses the Third to Sixth Dynasties, is often considered the golden age of Ancient Egypt. It was marked by the construction of the famous pyramids, including the Great Pyramid of Giza. The pharaohs held absolute power, and the centralized government was highly efficient.

3. **First Intermediate Period (c. 2181-2055 BCE):** During this time of political fragmentation and instability, power was decentralized, and different regions were ruled by local rulers. The First Intermediate Period is characterized by a decline in the central authority of the pharaoh and artistic expression.

4. **Middle Kingdom (c. 2055-1650 BCE):** This period, which covers the Eleventh and Twelfth Dynasties, saw the reunification of Egypt under a single ruler, Mentuhotep II. The Middle Kingdom was characterized by improved administration, territorial expansion, and artistic innovation.

5. **Second Intermediate Period (c. 1650-1550 BCE):** During this time, Egypt was again divided, with the Hyksos, a foreign group of people from Western Asia, ruling Lower Egypt. Meanwhile, the native Egyptian rulers controlled Upper Egypt.

6. **New Kingdom (c. 1550-1070 BCE):** Also known as the Egyptian Empire, this period saw the Eighteenth to Twentieth Dynasties of pharaohs. The New Kingdom was marked by a resurgence of Egyptian power and expansion, with famous pharaohs such as Hatshepsut, Akhenaten, Tutankhamun, and Ramesses II ruling during this time.

7. **Third Intermediate Period (c. 1070-664 BCE):** This period saw the decline of the central authority of the pharaohs, with Egypt again fragmented and ruled by various dynasties and foreign powers, including the

Nubians and the Libyans.

8. **Late Period (c. 664-332 BCE):** This period, marked by the Twenty-Sixth to the Thirtieth Dynasties, saw Egypt reestablish its independence after being controlled by foreign powers. However, the Persian Empire would eventually conquer Egypt in 525 BCE, marking the end of the Late Period.

9. **Greco-Roman Period (c. 332 BCE-395 CE):** Egypt became a province of the Macedonian Empire under Alexander the Great and later the Roman Empire. During this time, Greek and Roman culture had a significant influence on Egypt, but the traditional Egyptian culture persisted.

Now that you have an understanding of the different time periods these deities were worshipped within, let's become acquainted with the many gods and goddesses themselves.

Amun

Amun, also spelled as Amen or Amon, is a prominent god in ancient Egyptian mythology, initially associated with air and wind, and later known as the king of the gods and the god of creation. He is often depicted as a man wearing a double-plumed headdress and holding a scepter and ankh, symbolizing his authority and life-giving power.

Amun's worship dates back to the Old Kingdom, but his prominence significantly increased during the Middle Kingdom and the New Kingdom. His primary cult center was located in Thebes, where he was worshipped alongside the goddess Mut and their son, the moon god Khonsu, forming the Theban Triad.

During the New Kingdom, Amun's status rose to unprecedented heights, as he became closely associated with the pharaoh and the concept of divine kingship.

He was often referred to as the "Hidden One," reflecting his mysterious and powerful nature, and he was believed to have played a key role in the creation of the world.

Amun's influence further expanded when he was syncretized with the sun god Ra, forming Amun-Ra, a supreme god who combined the attributes of both deities. As Amun-Ra, he was considered the god of the sun, creation, and fertility, and he was revered as the ultimate source of life and divine power.

Throughout Egyptian history, Amun was a symbol of divine authority, protection, and creation. His importance in the Egyptian pantheon cannot be overstated, as he played a central role in the religious, political, and cultural life of ancient Egypt for centuries.

Ra (or Re)

Ra, also known as Re, is a central god in ancient Egyptian mythology, associated with the sun, creation, and kingship. He is often depicted as a man with the head of a falcon, wearing a solar disk encircled by a cobra (uraeus) on his head, or as a sun disk with the uraeus, symbolizing his power and connection to the sun.

Ra's worship dates back to the Predynastic Period, and his primary cult center was located in the city of Heliopolis. As the sun god, Ra was believed to travel across the sky each day on his solar barque, illuminating the world and providing life-giving energy to all creatures.

In Egyptian mythology, Ra played a crucial role in the creation of the world. According to the Heliopolitan creation myth, Ra emerged from the primordial waters of Nun as the first god, and he created other gods, including Shu (air) and Tefnut (moisture), who in turn gave birth to Geb (earth) and Nut (sky). As the creator god, Ra was considered the father of all gods and the source of life.

Ra was also closely associated with the concept of divine kingship, as the pharaoh was considered the living embodiment of Ra on earth. This association with the pharaoh and the sun reinforced the divine status and authority of the Egyptian ruler.

Throughout Egyptian history, Ra was revered as a powerful and life-sustaining deity, embodying the life-giving force of the sun and the creative power that brought forth the universe. His importance in the Egyptian pantheon is immense, as he influenced the religious and cultural life of ancient Egypt for millennia.

Atum

Atum, also known as Tem or Atem, is an important god in ancient Egyptian mythology, often associated with creation and the primeval force of the universe. Atum is depicted as a human wearing the double crown of Upper and Lower Egypt, symbolizing his role as a unifying force.

Atum was believed to be the first god and the prime mover of creation, representing both the sun and the completion of the cosmic cycle. He was sometimes associated with the setting sun, while Ra was associated with the rising sun. In this context, Atum embodied the ideas of completion, regeneration, and the beginning of a new day.

Horus

Horus is a prominent god in ancient Egyptian mythology, often depicted as a falcon or a man with a falcon's head wearing the double crown of Upper and Lower Egypt. As the god of the sky, he is closely associated with the sun and the moon, which were believed to be his right and left eyes, respectively.

Horus is the son of Osiris, the god of the afterlife, and Isis, the goddess of magic and healing. His story is central to the myth of Osiris, where he avenges his father's murder by battling his uncle Set, the god of chaos and storms. After a long struggle, Horus emerges victorious, restoring order to the cosmos and ascending to the throne as the rightful king of Egypt.

Horus symbolizes kingship, and ancient Egyptians believed that the pharaoh was the living embodiment of Horus on earth. As a protective deity, Horus was also invoked to safeguard the pharaoh and the people of Egypt. His story reflects themes of rebirth, the triumph of good over evil, and the cyclical nature of time.

Osiris

Osiris is a central figure in ancient Egyptian mythology, known as the god of the afterlife, the underworld, and resurrection. He is often depicted as a mummified man wearing the Atef crown, holding a crook and flail, symbols of kingship and authority.

Osiris is the son of Geb, the god of the earth, and Nut, the goddess of the sky. He is married to his sister, Isis, the goddess of magic and healing. In the Osiris myth, he becomes the first ruler of Egypt and brings civilization, agriculture, and law to the people. His brother Set, the god of chaos and storms, becomes envious of Osiris and eventually murders him. Isis, with the help of her sister Nephthys, recovers Osiris's body, and through her magic, temporarily brings him back to life to conceive their son, Horus.

Osiris then becomes the ruler of the underworld, where he judges the souls of the deceased, weighing their hearts against the feather of truth to determine their fate in the afterlife. His story represents themes of death, rebirth, and the triumph of order over chaos, and he is often invoked for protection and guidance during the journey to the afterlife.

Isis

Isis is a major goddess in ancient Egyptian mythology, known as the goddess of magic, healing, motherhood, and fertility. She is often depicted as a woman wearing a throne-shaped headdress or a vulture headdress with a solar disk between cow horns, symbolizing her role as a divine queen and mother.

Isis is the daughter of Geb, the god of the earth, and Nut, the goddess of the sky. She is married to her brother, Osiris, the god of the afterlife and the underworld.

Isis played a crucial role in the myth of Horus, raising and protecting him from Set until he was ready to challenge his uncle for the throne of Egypt. As a symbol of motherly devotion and protection, Isis became a popular deity among the Egyptian people. Her cult spread beyond Egypt's borders, and she was venerated throughout the Mediterranean region in the Greco-Roman period.

Set (or Seth)

Set, also known as Seth or Sutekh, is a complex and significant deity in ancient Egyptian mythology, associated with chaos, storms, deserts, and violence. He is often depicted as a man with the head of an unidentified, mythical creature called the Set animal, which has a long, curved snout and tall, squared-off ears.

Set is the son of Geb, the god of the earth, and Nut, the goddess of the sky. He is the brother of Osiris, Isis, and Nephthys.

Although Set was often vilified due to his role in the Osiris myth, he also had positive aspects in Egyptian mythology. He was considered a powerful protector and was sometimes depicted as the defender of the solar barque, repelling the serpent Apep, who sought to devour the sun. Throughout history, the perception of Set changed, and his role in the Egyptian pantheon evolved, reflecting the complex nature of this enigmatic deity.

Nephthys

Nephthys, also known as Nebthet or Nebet-Het, is an important goddess in ancient Egyptian mythology, associated with death, mourning, protection, and rebirth. She is often depicted as a woman wearing the hieroglyphic symbol for "house" on her head, or as a woman with falcon wings, symbolizing her protective nature.

Nephthys is the daughter of Geb, the god of the earth, and Nut, the goddess of the sky. She is the sister of Osiris, Isis, and Set, and is married to her brother Set. However, her allegiance lies with her sister Isis, and she plays a vital role in the Osiris myth.

Nephthys is also considered a protective deity of the dead, often depicted on funerary art and coffin texts, assisting the deceased in their journey through the afterlife. She is associated with the process of mummification and considered a companion to the souls during their passage into the underworld. As a goddess of mourning and protection, Nephthys provided comfort and guidance to both the living and the dead in ancient Egyptian beliefs.

Anubis

Anubis, also known as Inpu or Anpu, is a prominent god in ancient Egyptian mythology, associated with mummification, the afterlife, and the protection of tombs and cemeteries. He is often depicted as a man with the head of a jackal or as a full-bodied jackal, symbolizing his connection to the realms of death and the afterlife.

Anubis is the son of Osiris and Nephthys, although in some versions of the myth, he is considered the son of Ra. His primary role in Egyptian mythology is as the guardian and guide of the dead, responsible for overseeing the process of mummification and ensuring the proper burial rites are performed. Anubis is also an important figure in the weighing of the heart ceremony, where the heart of the deceased is weighed against the feather of truth, representing Ma'at, the goddess of truth and justice. Anubis's role is to ensure the scales are balanced and to guide the soul to its final judgment before Osiris, the ruler of the underworld.

As a god of protection, Anubis was revered for safeguarding tombs from thieves and desecration, as well as for his role in guiding and comforting the souls of the deceased during their journey through the afterlife.

Thoth

Thoth, also known as Djehuti or Tehuti, is a significant deity in ancient Egyptian mythology, associated with wisdom, writing, science, magic, and the moon. He is often depicted as a man with the head of an ibis or a baboon, both animals being sacred to him, and holding a writing palette and a reed pen, signifying his role as a scribe and keeper of knowledge.

Thoth is believed to be self-created or born from the head of Set, depending on the version of the myth. As the god of wisdom and knowledge, he played a vital role in maintaining the balance of the universe and was considered the inventor of writing, the creator of languages, and the scribe of the gods. Thoth was also the divine arbitrator, using his wisdom to settle disputes among the gods and maintain harmony in the cosmos.

Thoth played a crucial role in the restoration of the Eye of Horus after it was damaged during the battle between Horus and Set. He also assisted in the judgment of the dead, recording the results of the weighing of the heart ceremony, and ensuring the proper execution of divine justice. Thoth was revered as a patron of scribes, scholars, and knowledge seekers, and his influence extended into the realms of magic, medicine, and the sciences.

Ma'at

Ma'at is a central goddess in ancient Egyptian mythology, representing the concepts of truth, justice, balance, harmony, and cosmic order. She is often depicted as a woman wearing an ostrich feather on her head, which is the hieroglyphic symbol for her name and the embodiment of the principles she represents.

Ma'at is believed to be the daughter of Ra, the sun god, and is closely associated with the maintenance of the balance and order of the universe. According to Egyptian beliefs, the world was created and sustained by Ma'at, and her presence was essential for the functioning of the cosmos and the well-being of society.

In Egyptian mythology, Ma'at plays a critical role in the judgment of the dead during the weighing of the heart ceremony. The heart of the deceased is weighed against the feather of Ma'at to determine if the person lived a righteous life in accordance with the principles of truth and justice. If the heart is found to be lighter than the feather, the soul is allowed to proceed into the afterlife; if the heart is heavier, it is devoured by the monstrous Ammit, and the soul is denied eternal life.

Ma'at was not only a goddess but also a concept that permeated Egyptian life, signifying the importance of living in harmony with both the divine and the earthly realms. The pharaohs were considered the guardians of Ma'at and were responsible for ensuring that her principles guided the administration of the country.

Ptah

Ptah is a significant god in ancient Egyptian mythology, associated with creation, craftsmanship, and the arts. He is often depicted as a mummified man wearing a skullcap, holding a staff that combines the symbols of power, life, and stability (the was-scepter, ankh, and djed pillar).

Ptah is considered the chief deity of the city of Memphis, and in the Memphite creation myth, he is regarded as the creator of the universe. According to this myth, Ptah created the world and all living beings through the power of his thoughts and words. He first conceived the divine ideas in his heart and then spoke them into existence, manifesting the physical world and the gods.

As the god of craftsmanship and the arts, Ptah was the patron of artisans, architects, and builders, who invoked his guidance and protection in their work. He was believed to have designed and built the divine structures in the heavens and the underworld, as well as the mortal realm. Additionally, Ptah was associated with the rejuvenation and regeneration of the world, ensuring its continuous existence through the power of his creative force.

Throughout Egyptian history, Ptah was revered as a central deity, and his cult was particularly influential in the city of Memphis, where he was often worshipped alongside his consort Sekhmet and their son Nefertum.

Hathor

Hathor is a prominent goddess in ancient Egyptian mythology, associated with love, fertility, motherhood, beauty, and music. She is often depicted as a cow, a woman with the head of a cow, or a woman wearing a headdress featuring cow horns and a solar disk, emphasizing her connection to motherhood and nourishment.

Hathor is considered the daughter of Ra, the sun god, although in some myths she is associated with other gods, such as Horus or Ptah. As a celestial goddess, she was believed to be the mother of the sky and the embodiment of the Milky Way, providing nourishment to the cosmos.

In Egyptian mythology, Hathor had both nurturing and destructive aspects. She was revered as a goddess of love, beauty, and joy, who blessed the living with happiness and protected women during childbirth. She also had a strong association with music and dance, and her priestesses were known for their musical skills and performances in her honor.

However, Hathor was also linked to the myth of the Eye of Ra, in which she took on a fierce, lioness form known as Sekhmet to punish humanity for their disobedience to the sun god. After a rampage that almost annihilated humanity, she was eventually appeased by being tricked into drinking beer, which she mistook for blood, and returned to her gentle, nurturing form.

Hathor was widely worshipped throughout ancient Egypt, and her cult extended beyond its borders into the broader Mediterranean region. As a goddess of many aspects, she played a significant role in the daily lives of the Egyptians and was invoked for protection, love, and joy.

Geb

Geb is an important god in ancient Egyptian mythology, associated with the earth, fertility, and agriculture. He is often depicted as a man with a goose on his head or as a man lying down beneath the arch of the sky goddess Nut, symbolizing his role as the earth deity and his connection to the heavens.

Geb is the son of Shu, the god of air, and Tefnut, the goddess of moisture. He is the brother and husband of Nut, the goddess of the sky, and together they form a divine pair representing the union of earth and sky. They are the parents of Osiris, Isis, Set, and Nephthys, who are central figures in the Egyptian pantheon and mythology.

In Egyptian myths, Geb plays a key role in the creation story, where he emerges as a result of the separation of the primordial waters by the sun god Ra. After their father Shu lifts Nut into the sky, Geb remains as the earth god, responsible for the fertility of the land and the growth of crops. His laughter was believed to cause earthquakes, emphasizing his connection to the forces of nature.

As an earth deity, Geb was closely associated with the afterlife and was believed to provide a resting place for the deceased. He was invoked in funerary texts and rituals to ensure a fertile and productive afterlife for the dead. Throughout Egyptian history, Geb was revered as a guardian of the earth, the source of life and abundance, and a protector of the deceased.

Nut

Nut is a prominent goddess in ancient Egyptian mythology, associated with the sky, the cosmos, and the celestial bodies. She is often depicted as a woman arched over the earth god Geb, her body adorned with stars, symbolizing her role as the canopy of the sky and the mother of the celestial bodies.

Nut is the daughter of Shu, the god of air, and Tefnut, the goddess of moisture. She is the sister and wife of Geb, the earth god, and together they form a divine pair representing the union of earth and sky. They are the parents of Osiris, Isis, Seth, and Nephthys, who are central figures in the Egyptian pantheon and mythology.

In Egyptian creation myths, Nut is a key figure, emerging as a result of the separation of the primordial waters by the sun god Ra. After being lifted into the sky by her father Shu, she becomes the sky goddess, responsible for the heavenly bodies and the cycle of day and night. Nut is also believed to give birth to the sun each morning and swallow it each evening, emphasizing her role in the cosmic cycle.

As a sky deity, Nut was closely associated with the afterlife, providing a celestial home for the souls of the deceased. She was often invoked in funerary texts and rituals to ensure the protection and guidance of the dead in their journey through the afterlife. Throughout Egyptian history, Nut was revered as the mother of the cosmos, the guardian of the celestial realm, and a protector of the deceased.

Sobek

Sobek, also known as Sebek or Suchos, is a prominent god in ancient Egyptian mythology, associated with the Nile crocodile, fertility, military prowess, and protection. He is often depicted as a man with the head of a crocodile or as a full-bodied crocodile, symbolizing his connection to the powerful and feared Nile crocodile.

The origins of Sobek's worship can be traced back to the Old Kingdom, and his cult centers were mainly located in the Faiyum region and at Kom Ombo, where a double temple was dedicated to him and the god Horus. In some myths, Sobek is considered the son of Neith, the goddess of war and hunting, emphasizing his association with military prowess and protection.

In Egyptian mythology, Sobek was seen as a protective and nurturing deity. He was believed to have aided in the creation of the world by emerging from the primordial waters and laying eggs on the bank, which then hatched into the world. As a fertility god, Sobek was associated with the life-giving waters of the Nile, and his annual appearance in the river was thought to coincide with the beginning of the Nile flood, a crucial event for Egyptian agriculture.

Sobek was also a protective deity, known for safeguarding the pharaoh and the Egyptian people from the dangers of the Nile and its inhabitants. His ferocious and powerful nature was both feared and respected, and he was invoked for protection in various aspects of daily life, including during times of war and conflict.

Tefnut

Tefnut is an important goddess in ancient Egyptian mythology, associated with moisture, dew, rain, and fertility. She is often depicted as a woman with the head of a lioness, wearing a solar disk and a uraeus, or as a full-bodied lioness, reflecting her fierce and powerful nature.

Tefnut is a key figure in the Egyptian creation myth, as she is one of the first gods created by the sun god, Ra (or Atum, in some versions). According to the myth, Ra created Tefnut and her twin brother Shu, the god of air, by either sneezing or through his own semen, depending on the version of the story. As the goddess of moisture, Tefnut plays a crucial role in sustaining life on earth, as her union with Shu brings forth the life-giving elements of air and moisture.

Tefnut and Shu are the parents of Geb, the earth god, and Nut, the sky goddess, who in turn give birth to the divine siblings Osiris, Isis, Set, and Nephthys. Tefnut's connection to the primordial waters and the natural world underscores her importance in the Egyptian pantheon.

Throughout Egyptian history, Tefnut was revered as a nurturing and life-sustaining goddess, whose powers were essential to the survival of the natural world and the human race. She was also a symbol of the interconnectedness of the elements, emphasizing the delicate balance that maintained life and order in the cosmos.

Shu

Shu is a significant god in ancient Egyptian mythology, associated with air, light, and the space between the earth and the sky. He is often depicted as a man wearing an ostrich feather on his head or holding a scepter and ankh, symbolizing his role as a life-giving force and his connection to the air.

Shu is a key figure in the Egyptian creation myth, as he is one of the first gods created by the sun god, Ra (or Atum, in some versions).

Shu and Tefnut are the parents of Geb, the earth god, and Nut, the sky goddess. In Egyptian mythology, Shu is responsible for separating Geb and Nut, lifting Nut into the sky to create the space between the earth and the heavens. This separation allows for the creation of the world and its inhabitants, emphasizing Shu's importance in the formation of the cosmos.

Throughout Egyptian history, Shu was revered as a life-sustaining and protective deity, whose powers were essential for the survival of the natural world.

Khnum

Khnum is an ancient god in Egyptian mythology, associated with the Nile, fertility, creation, and pottery. He is often depicted as a man with the head of a ram, holding a potter's wheel, or as a full-bodied ram, symbolizing his connection to fertility and creative power.

Khnum is believed to be one of the oldest Egyptian deities, with his worship dating back to the Predynastic Period. His primary cult centers were located on the island of Elephantine and at Esna, where he was often worshipped alongside other deities related to the Nile and fertility.

In Egyptian mythology, Khnum was regarded as a creator god, responsible for molding humans and animals out of clay before placing them in their mother's womb. He was believed to have created the first human couple, as well as the bodies of the gods. Using his potter's wheel, Khnum shaped each individual's body and determined their destiny, emphasizing his role as a life-giving force.

Additionally, Khnum was closely associated with the Nile, particularly its source and the annual inundation that was crucial for Egyptian agriculture. He was believed to control the flow of the Nile and its life-giving waters, which he used to nourish the land and its inhabitants. Throughout Egyptian history, Khnum was revered as a benevolent and creative deity, who played a crucial role in the formation of life and the sustenance of the natural world.

Hapi

Hapi is a prominent god in ancient Egyptian mythology, associated with the Nile River, fertility, and abundance. He is often depicted as a well-fed man with large breasts and a round belly, symbolizing his connection to fertility and nourishment. He is also shown with aquatic plants, such as papyrus and lotus, emphasizing his association with the Nile.

Hapi is not to be confused with the god of the same name in ancient Egyptian funerary texts, who was one of the Four Sons of Horus and was responsible for protecting the deceased's organs. The Hapi discussed here is specifically the god of the Nile.

In Egyptian mythology, Hapi was regarded as the personification of the Nile River and its annual flood, which was essential for the fertility and prosperity of the land. The Nile's floodwaters deposited fertile silt along its banks, enabling the growth of crops and supporting the livelihood of the Egyptian people. As a result, Hapi was worshipped and celebrated for his life-giving powers and his role in ensuring the success of agriculture.

There were two aspects of Hapi – one representing the Nile's source in Upper Egypt and the other representing its source in Lower Egypt. Each aspect had its own set of rituals and offerings to ensure the god's continued favor and the fertility of the land.

Throughout Egyptian history, Hapi was revered as a benevolent and nurturing deity who played a vital role in the survival and prosperity of the Egyptian people.

His annual flood was eagerly anticipated and celebrated, as it was seen as a divine blessing that ensured the fertility of the land and the well-being of its inhabitants.

Bastet (or Bast)

Bastet, also known as Bast, is an important goddess in ancient Egyptian mythology, associated with protection, fertility, motherhood, and domestic cats. She is often depicted as a woman with the head of a lioness or a domestic cat, wearing a solar disk and a uraeus, or as a full-bodied cat or lioness, symbolizing her protective and nurturing qualities.

Bastet's worship dates back to the Second Dynasty, and her primary cult center was located in the city of Bubastis in the Nile Delta. Over time, her portrayal evolved from a fierce lioness goddess to a gentler domestic cat deity, reflecting the changing beliefs and priorities of the Egyptian people.

In Egyptian mythology, Bastet was considered the daughter of the sun god Ra, and she played a crucial role in defending him from his enemies, such as the serpent Apep. As a protective deity, Bastet was believed to guard the home and family, as well as the pharaoh and the nation. Her close association with cats, which were highly valued in ancient Egyptian society for their ability to protect homes from vermin and snakes, further emphasized her protective qualities.

Additionally, Bastet was associated with fertility and motherhood, and she was often invoked to protect pregnant women and ensure the health and well-being of their children. As a nurturing and caring goddess, she was revered by the Egyptian people, who celebrated her in an annual festival that was one of the most popular and elaborate in ancient Egypt.

Throughout Egyptian history, Bastet was a symbol of protection, fertility, and domesticity, embodying the qualities that were essential for the preservation of life and the stability of the home and the nation.

Sekhmet

Sekhmet is a powerful goddess in ancient Egyptian mythology, associated with war, destruction, healing, and the fierce heat of the sun. She is often depicted as a woman with the head of a lioness, wearing a solar disk and a uraeus, or as a full-bodied lioness, symbolizing her ferocious and fearsome nature.

Sekhmet's worship dates back to the Old Kingdom, and her primary cult center was located in Memphis, where she was considered the consort of the creator god Ptah and the mother of the lotus god Nefertem. She was also worshipped in Thebes alongside the god Amun and the goddess Mut.

In Egyptian mythology, Sekhmet is considered the daughter of the sun god Ra and is believed to have been created from his fiery eye to punish humanity for their disobedience. In the myth, Sekhmet becomes uncontrollable, nearly destroying all of humanity before Ra intervenes and tricks her into drinking beer dyed red to resemble blood, causing her to become intoxicated and fall asleep, thus saving the human race.

Despite her destructive and fierce nature, Sekhmet was also associated with healing, and she was considered a powerful protector against diseases and evil forces. As the "Mistress of Life" and the "Lady of Pestilence," she had the power to both cause and cure illness, and many Egyptian physicians invoked her for protection and guidance.

Throughout Egyptian history, Sekhmet was revered as a powerful and complex deity who embodied both the destructive and healing aspects of the natural world. Her dual nature made her a symbol of the balance and harmony that maintained life and order in the cosmos.

Neith

Neith is an ancient goddess in Egyptian mythology, associated with war, hunting, weaving, and creation. She is often depicted as a woman wearing the red crown of Lower Egypt, holding a bow and arrows, or as a woman with the emblem of two crossed arrows over a shield, symbolizing her connection to warfare and hunting.

Neith's worship dates back to the Predynastic Period, making her one of the oldest Egyptian deities. Her primary cult center was located in the city of Sais in the Nile Delta, where she was considered the patron goddess and was highly revered.

In Egyptian mythology, Neith played a unique role as a creator goddess. According to some creation myths, she was considered the mother of the sun god Ra, while in others, she was believed to have created the world by weaving it into existence. As a creator, she was sometimes referred to as the "Great Cow" who gave birth to the universe.

Neith was also associated with the protection of the dead, and she was believed to guard the canopic jars containing the organs of the deceased, alongside the goddess Serket. As a funerary deity, she played a crucial role in the afterlife, ensuring the well-being and protection of the dead.

Throughout Egyptian history, Neith was revered as a powerful and versatile deity, embodying the qualities of both a warrior and a creator, as well as a guardian of the dead. Her worship spanned across millennia, reflecting her enduring significance in the religious and cultural life of ancient Egypt.

Wadjet

Wadjet, also spelled as Uadjet or Wedjat, is an ancient goddess in Egyptian mythology, associated with protection, royalty, and the unification of Lower Egypt. She is often depicted as a cobra, sometimes wearing the Red Crown of Lower Egypt, or as a lion-headed woman, symbolizing her protective qualities and connection to the Egyptian monarchy.

Wadjet's worship dates back to the Predynastic Period, and her primary cult center was located in the city of Buto in the Nile Delta. As the patron goddess of Lower Egypt, she played a significant role in the unification of Upper and Lower Egypt, alongside her counterpart Nekhbet, the vulture goddess and patron of Upper Egypt.

In Egyptian mythology, Wadjet was considered the protector of the pharaoh and the daughter of the sun god Ra. As a cobra, she was believed to spit fire at the pharaoh's enemies, and she was often depicted on the royal headdress as a symbol of the pharaoh's divine authority and protection. The Eye of Horus, also known as the Eye of Wadjet, is a powerful protective amulet in ancient Egyptian culture, believed to embody the protective powers of the goddess.

Throughout Egyptian history, Wadjet was revered as a symbol of protection, royalty, and the unity of Egypt. Her association with the pharaoh and her protective powers made her a significant figure in the religious and political life of ancient Egypt, and her influence can still be seen in the form of the Eye of Horus amulet, which remains a popular symbol of protection and good fortune today.

Nekhbet

Nekhbet is an ancient goddess in Egyptian mythology, associated with protection, royalty, and the unification of Upper Egypt. She is often depicted as a vulture, sometimes wearing the White Crown of Upper Egypt, or as a woman with the head of a vulture, symbolizing her protective qualities and connection to the Egyptian monarchy.

Nekhbet's worship dates back to the Predynastic Period, and her primary cult center was located in the city of Nekheb (El Kab) in Upper Egypt. As the patron goddess of Upper Egypt, she played a significant role in the unification of Upper and Lower Egypt, alongside her counterpart Wadjet, the cobra goddess and patron of Lower Egypt.

In Egyptian mythology, Nekhbet was considered the protector of the pharaoh and was often referred to as the "Mother of Mothers." As a vulture, she was believed to provide a nurturing and protective presence, and she was often depicted on the royal headdress, with her wings outstretched, as a symbol of the pharaoh's divine authority and protection.

Together with Wadjet, Nekhbet formed the "Two Ladies," a title representing the united power and authority of the pharaoh over both Upper and Lower Egypt. The Two Ladies were often depicted on the royal insignia, such as the serekh and the nemes headdress, symbolizing the unity and stability of the Egyptian state.

Throughout Egyptian history, Nekhbet was revered as a symbol of protection, royalty, and the unity of Egypt. Her association with the pharaoh and her protective powers made her a significant figure in the religious and political life of ancient Egypt, as she embodied the ideals of divine kingship and the harmony of the Egyptian state.

Seshat

Seshat is an ancient goddess in Egyptian mythology, associated with wisdom, writing, knowledge, and measurement. She is often depicted as a woman wearing a leopard-skin dress and a headdress with a seven-pointed emblem, which represents a stylized papyrus plant, symbolizing her connection to writing and knowledge.

Seshat's worship dates back to the Early Dynastic Period, and although she did not have a specific cult center, she was revered throughout Egypt as the goddess of scribes and the patroness of libraries and archives.

In Egyptian mythology, Seshat played a crucial role as the divine record-keeper and the guardian of sacred knowledge. She was considered the inventor of writing, and it was believed that she taught this skill to humanity. As a goddess of measurement, she was also responsible for laying out the foundations of temples and other sacred buildings, ensuring their precise alignment with the cosmos.

Seshat was closely associated with the pharaoh, assisting him in the "Stretching of the Cord" ceremony, a ritual performed to establish the dimensions of a temple before construction. In this ceremony, Seshat used her knowledge of geometry and her divine powers to ensure the accurate placement and alignment of the temple, symbolizing the harmony between the earthly and celestial realms.

Throughout Egyptian history, Seshat was revered as a symbol of wisdom, knowledge, and divine order. Her association with writing, measurement, and sacred architecture made her a significant figure in the religious and cultural life of ancient Egypt, embodying the ideals of learning and the preservation of knowledge for future generations.

Khepri

Khepri is an ancient god in Egyptian mythology, associated with the sun, creation, and rebirth. He is often depicted as a scarab beetle, or as a man with the head of a scarab, symbolizing his connection to the rising sun and the process of transformation.

The worship of Khepri dates back to the Old Kingdom, and although he did not have a specific cult center, he was revered throughout Egypt as a manifestation of the sun god, Ra.

In Egyptian mythology, Khepri played a significant role in the daily cycle of the sun. He was believed to represent the morning aspect of the sun god, responsible for pushing the sun across the sky each day, just as a scarab beetle rolls a ball of dung, which it uses for food and reproduction. This association with the scarab beetle and the sun emphasized the concepts of creation, transformation, and renewal in Khepri's symbolism.

Khepri was also associated with the process of rebirth, as the scarab beetle was believed to be spontaneously generated from the dung ball it rolled, reflecting the idea of life emerging from death. This connection to rebirth made Khepri an important symbol of the afterlife and the resurrection of the deceased.

Throughout Egyptian history, Khepri was revered as a symbol of the sun's daily journey, creation, and renewal. His association with the scarab beetle and the rising sun made him a significant figure in the religious and cultural life of ancient Egypt, embodying the ideals of transformation and the cyclical nature of life.

Bes

Bes is a unique and popular god in ancient Egyptian mythology, associated with protection, fertility, childbirth, and the home. He is often depicted as a dwarf with a lion-like or leonine face, a beard, and a protruding tongue, wearing a plumed headdress and sometimes holding musical instruments or weapons.

Bes's worship dates back to the Old Kingdom, and while he did not have a specific cult center, his popularity was widespread throughout Egypt. He was particularly venerated in households, where his protective nature was believed to ward off evil spirits and bring good fortune.

In Egyptian mythology, Bes played a significant role in protecting and nurturing families, especially women and children. He was considered a guardian against malevolent forces, such as evil spirits, dangerous animals, and diseases. Bes was also associated with music and dance, believed to use these arts to drive away evil and create a joyful atmosphere.

Bes was often invoked during childbirth to protect both the mother and the newborn child. His protective qualities extended to fertility, and he was believed to ensure the well-being and prosperity of the family.

Throughout Egyptian history, Bes was revered as a symbol of protection, joy, and the well-being of families. His unique appearance and role in the everyday lives of the Egyptians made him a beloved figure in the religious and cultural life of ancient Egypt, embodying the ideals of happiness, safety, and prosperity within the home.

Taweret (or Taurt)

Taweret, also known as Taurt or Taueret, is a goddess in ancient Egyptian mythology, associated with protection, fertility, and childbirth. She is often depicted as a bipedal female hippopotamus with the limbs and tail of a lion, and the back and mane of a crocodile, emphasizing her protective nature and connection to the dangerous animals of the Nile.

Taweret's worship dates back to the Old Kingdom, and while she did not have a specific cult center, her popularity was widespread throughout Egypt. She was particularly venerated in households, where her protective nature was believed to ensure the well-being of pregnant women and their unborn children.

In Egyptian mythology, Taweret played a significant role in safeguarding women during pregnancy and childbirth. She was considered a guardian against malevolent forces that could threaten the well-being of mothers and their babies, and she was invoked for protection during labor. Taweret was also associated with fertility, as her connection to the nurturing and protective aspects of the Nile's fauna made her a symbol of life and abundance.

Throughout Egyptian history, Taweret was revered as a symbol of protection, fertility, and the well-being of expectant mothers and their children. Her unique appearance and role in the everyday lives of the Egyptians made her an important figure in the religious and cultural life of ancient Egypt, embodying the ideals of nurturing, safety, and the sanctity of motherhood.

Apep (or Apophis)

Apep, also known as Apophis, is an ancient god and malevolent entity in Egyptian mythology, associated with chaos, darkness, and destruction. Apep is often depicted as a giant serpent, sometimes with wings, emphasizing his sinister nature and his role as the eternal enemy of the sun god, Ra.

Apep's origins can be traced back to the Middle Kingdom, and though he did not have a specific cult center, he was widely feared throughout Egypt as the embodiment of chaos and disorder, opposing the principles of harmony and balance represented by Ma'at.

In Egyptian mythology, Apep played a significant role as the primary antagonist in the daily journey of the sun god, Ra, through the underworld. Each night, as Ra traveled through the twelve hours of darkness in his solar barque, Apep would attempt to devour the sun and plunge the world into eternal darkness. Ra, accompanied by a host of protective deities, would battle Apep, using spells and weapons to repel the chaos serpent and ensure the sun's triumphant rise the next morning.

This mythological struggle between Ra and Apep symbolized the cosmic battle between order and chaos, a central theme in ancient Egyptian religion. The daily triumph of Ra over Apep represented the victory of order, light, and life over disorder, darkness, and destruction.

Throughout Egyptian history, Apep was feared and reviled as the embodiment of chaos and the enemy of order. His eternal conflict with Ra reflected the ancient Egyptians' understanding of the delicate balance between the forces of harmony and chaos, and the importance of maintaining that balance in both the cosmic and earthly realms.

Khonsu

Khonsu is an ancient god in Egyptian mythology, associated with the moon, time, and healing. He is often depicted as a young man with a falcon's head wearing a lunar disk and crescent moon on his head, symbolizing his connection to the moon and its cycles.

Khonsu's worship dates back to the New Kingdom, with his primary cult center located in Thebes, where he was part of the Theban Triad along with his father, Amun, and his mother, Mut. This triad of deities was highly significant in the religious life of Thebes and played a central role in the state religion.

In Egyptian mythology, Khonsu played a significant role as the god of the moon and time. As a lunar deity, he was responsible for regulating the lunar cycle, which was essential for the ancient Egyptians' calendar system and religious festivals. The moon was also associated with growth and fertility, and Khonsu was sometimes invoked to ensure the well-being of crops and livestock.

Khonsu was also revered as a god of healing and was believed to possess the power to drive away evil spirits and protect against illness. This aspect of his nature made him a popular deity for individuals seeking relief from ailments or protection from harm.

Throughout Egyptian history, Khonsu was revered as a symbol of the moon, time, and healing. His association with the Theban Triad and his protective qualities made him an important figure in the religious and cultural life of ancient Egypt, embodying the ideals of growth, fertility, and well-being.

Montu

Montu is an ancient god in Egyptian mythology, associated with war, strength, and valor. He is often depicted as a falcon-headed or a bull-headed man wearing the double-plumed headdress with a sun disk, emphasizing his connection to the sun and his martial nature.

Montu's worship dates back to the Middle Kingdom, with his primary cult center located in Thebes, where he was venerated as the city's patron deity before the rise of the Theban Triad. Montu also had important temples in Armant, Medamud, and Karnak, which further solidified his status as a prominent god in ancient Egypt.

In Egyptian mythology, Montu played a significant role as the god of war and a divine protector of the pharaoh. Montu was believed to grant the pharaoh strength and courage in battle, ensuring victory over their enemies. As a warrior god, Montu was also associated with the fierceness and power of the bull, an animal symbolizing strength and virility in ancient Egyptian culture.

The pharaohs often sought Montu's favor, invoking his name and wearing his symbols in their military campaigns. This connection between Montu and the pharaoh was especially strong during the New Kingdom when the Egyptian empire expanded and engaged in numerous conflicts.

Throughout Egyptian history, Montu was revered as a symbol of strength, courage, and military prowess. His association with the sun and the warrior aspect made him an important figure in the religious and cultural life of ancient Egypt, embodying the ideals of divine protection and the victorious power of the pharaoh in battle.

Anhur (or Onuris)

Anhur, also known as Onuris or Inhert, is an ancient god in Egyptian mythology, associated with war, hunting, and the sun. He is often depicted as a tall, bearded man wearing a long kilt and a headdress with four tall feathers, carrying a spear or a lance, emphasizing his martial nature and connection to the sun.

Anhur's worship dates back to the Middle Kingdom, with his primary cult center located in the city of Thinis in Upper Egypt. Over time, his popularity and influence extended throughout Egypt, making him an important deity in the Egyptian pantheon.

In Egyptian mythology, Anhur played a significant role as a god of war and a divine protector. He was believed to embody the strength and courage required in battle, ensuring victory for the Egyptian armies. As a hunter god, Anhur was also associated with the act of chasing and capturing enemies, making him a symbol of triumph over chaos and disorder.

Additionally, Anhur was connected to the sun god, Ra, and was sometimes regarded as the son of Ra, further highlighting his solar associations. In this capacity, Anhur was seen as a defender of the sun god and a guardian against the forces of chaos that threatened to disrupt the cosmic order.

Throughout Egyptian history, Anhur was revered as a symbol of strength, courage, and military skill. His association with war, hunting, and the sun made him an important figure in the religious and cultural life of ancient Egypt, embodying the ideals of divine protection and the victorious power of the Egyptian armies.

Mut

Mut is an ancient goddess in Egyptian mythology, associated with motherhood, fertility, and protection. She is often depicted as a woman wearing the double crown of Upper and Lower Egypt or the vulture headdress, symbolizing her role as a divine mother and her connection to the rulership of Egypt.

Mut's worship dates back to the Middle Kingdom, with her primary cult center located in Thebes, where she was part of the Theban Triad along with her husband, Amun, and her son, Khonsu. This triad of deities was highly significant in the religious life of Thebes and played a central role in the state religion.

In Egyptian mythology, Mut played a significant role as a mother goddess and a protector of the pharaoh. As the wife of Amun, the king of the gods, she was considered the queen of the gods and was often associated with the divine motherhood of the pharaoh. Mut was also believed to embody the protective and nurturing qualities of a mother, and she was invoked to safeguard the pharaoh and ensure the stability of the kingdom.

Mut was sometimes depicted as a lioness or as a woman with a lion's head, highlighting her fierce protective nature and her connection to the powerful leonine goddesses of ancient Egypt, such as Sekhmet and Bastet.

Throughout Egyptian history, Mut was revered as a symbol of motherhood, fertility, and divine protection. Her association with the Theban Triad and her role as the divine mother of the pharaoh made her an important figure in the religious and cultural life of ancient Egypt, embodying the ideals of nurturing, safety, and the sanctity of motherhood.

Min

Min is an ancient god in Egyptian mythology, associated with fertility, male sexuality, and the creative force of nature. He is often depicted as a man with an erect phallus, holding a flail, and wearing a double-plumed headdress or a crown with tall plumes, symbolizing his connection to fertility and power.

Min's worship dates back to the Predynastic Period, with his primary cult center located in the city of Coptos (modern-day Qift) in Upper Egypt. His importance in the Egyptian pantheon is evident from his early association with the pharaoh's power and the fertility of the land.

In Egyptian mythology, Min played a significant role as a god of fertility, ensuring the abundance of crops and the procreation of people and animals. As a symbol of virility and the generative power of nature, Min was often invoked during agricultural and fertility rites, with festivals held in his honor to ensure the prosperity of the land.

Min was also associated with the eastern desert and its resources, such as precious metals and valuable stones, further emphasizing his role in ensuring abundance and wealth. Additionally, Min was sometimes linked to the lunar cycle and the waxing moon, which in turn, were associated with growth and fertility.

Throughout Egyptian history, Min was revered as a symbol of fertility, abundance, and the creative force of nature. His association with agriculture, procreation, and natural resources made him an important figure in the religious and cultural life of ancient Egypt, embodying the ideals of growth, prosperity, and the regenerative powers of the natural world.

Meretseger

Meretseger, meaning "She Who Loves Silence," is an ancient goddess in Egyptian mythology, associated with protection, guardianship, and the divine embodiment of the local landscape. She is often depicted as a cobra, a woman with a cobra's head, or a woman with a scorpion on her head, symbolizing her role as a fierce protector and her connection to the natural world.

Meretseger's worship is primarily linked to the area surrounding the Valley of the Kings and the workers' village of Deir el-Medina, which dates back to the New Kingdom. As the patron deity of the necropolis, she was responsible for guarding the tombs of the pharaohs and protecting them from grave robbers and other threats.

In Egyptian mythology, Meretseger played a significant role as a guardian goddess and protector of the necropolis. She was believed to inhabit the local hills, particularly the pyramid-shaped peak overlooking the Valley of the Kings, which was considered her divine embodiment. Meretseger's protective nature extended not only to the tombs of the pharaohs but also to the workers and artisans living in Deir el-Medina, who were responsible for constructing and decorating the royal tombs.

As a goddess connected to the natural landscape, Meretseger was also associated with the local flora and fauna, particularly the venomous snakes and scorpions that inhabited the desert region. Her ability to inflict or cure venomous bites further highlighted her dual nature as both a dangerous and nurturing deity.

Throughout Egyptian history, Meretseger was revered as a symbol of protection, guardianship, and the divine embodiment of the local landscape. Her association with the Valley of the Kings and her role as a fierce protector made her an important figure in the religious and cultural life of the ancient Egyptians, particularly for those living and working in the vicinity of the royal necropolis.

Qetesh

Qetesh, also spelled Qudshu or Kadesh, is a goddess in ancient Egyptian mythology, associated with love, sexuality, beauty, and fertility. Qetesh is believed to have originated from the Levant, and her worship was integrated into the Egyptian pantheon during the New Kingdom, when Egypt had extensive interactions with the Near Eastern cultures.

Qetesh is often depicted as a beautiful, nude woman standing or riding a lion, holding a snake in one hand and a bouquet of lotus flowers in the other. These symbols emphasize her connection to love, sensuality, and the beauty of nature. She is also occasionally shown wearing the headdress of Hathor, highlighting the association between the two goddesses.

In Egyptian mythology, Qetesh played a role as a goddess of love, sexuality, and fertility, embodying the sensual aspects of life and the generative power of nature. Her worship, which included rituals and offerings, was aimed at invoking her blessings for love, passion, and fertility in both human lives and the natural world.

Qetesh's association with other goddesses of love, such as Hathor and the Canaanite goddess Astarte, reflects the syncretic nature of ancient Egyptian religion, as various deities from different cultures were incorporated and assimilated into the Egyptian pantheon.

Throughout Egyptian history, Qetesh was revered as a symbol of love, sexuality, and fertility. Her connection to the sensual aspects of life and the natural world made her an important figure in the religious and cultural life of ancient Egypt, embodying the ideals of passion, beauty, and the generative powers of nature.

Mafdet

Mafdet is an early goddess in Egyptian mythology, associated with protection, justice, and the execution of evil forces. She is often depicted as a feline or a mongoose, which were both revered for their skill in killing snakes and other venomous creatures. Mafdet's imagery and role reflect her connection to the natural world and her protective nature.

Mafdet's worship dates back to the Early Dynastic Period and continued throughout the Old Kingdom. Although her cult was later overshadowed by other feline goddesses like Bastet and Sekhmet, Mafdet retained her significance as a protective deity in religious texts and iconography.

In Egyptian mythology, Mafdet played a significant role as a guardian and protector against evil forces, particularly snakes and scorpions, which were considered embodiments of chaos and disorder. Mafdet's protective nature extended to the pharaoh and the common people, as well as safeguarding the sacred spaces of temples and tombs.

Mafdet was also associated with justice and the execution of wrongdoers. Her connection to the natural world and her ability to defeat venomous creatures made her an ideal symbol for the triumph of order over chaos. In the Pyramid Texts, Mafdet was described as a powerful force, running up the pharaoh's staff to decapitate his enemies.

Throughout Egyptian history, Mafdet was revered as a symbol of protection, justice, and the defeat of evil forces. Her association with the natural world and her role as a guardian and protector made her an important figure in the religious and cultural life of ancient Egypt, embodying the ideals of order, balance, and the triumph of good over evil.

Babi

Babi, also known as Baba, is a lesser-known deity in Egyptian mythology, associated with aggression, violence, and male sexuality. He is often depicted as a baboon or a man with the head of a baboon, reflecting his connection to the natural world and the aggressive behavior of these animals.

Babi's worship dates back to the Old Kingdom, although his cult was not as prominent as those of other baboon-related deities such as Thoth and Hapi. Babi's role in the Egyptian pantheon is primarily focused on his violent and aggressive aspects, which were both feared and revered by the ancient Egyptians.

In Egyptian mythology, Babi played a significant role as a symbol of primal, uncontrollable aggression and power. He was considered a dangerous and unpredictable deity, embodying the darker aspects of human nature and the natural world. Babi's association with male sexuality also linked him to virility and fertility, further emphasizing his connection to the generative power of nature.

Babi's aggressive and violent nature also extended to the afterlife. In some funerary texts, he is depicted as a guardian of the deceased's soul, using his aggressive behavior to ward off malevolent spirits and ensure the safe passage of the deceased through the underworld.

Throughout Egyptian history, Babi was revered as a symbol of aggression, violence, and male sexuality. His connection to the natural world and the darker aspects of human nature made him an important, albeit lesser-known, figure in the religious and cultural life of ancient Egypt, embodying the raw power and uncontrollable energy of the animal kingdom.

Heka

Heka, in Egyptian mythology, is the personification of magic and the power of divine forces. The term "heka" also refers to the practice of magic itself in ancient Egypt. Heka, as a deity, is often depicted as a man carrying a staff entwined with two serpents, symbolizing the dual aspects of his power – creation and destruction. In some representations, Heka wears the sidelock of youth, associating him with the child form of the sun god, Ra.

The concept of Heka dates back to the Early Dynastic Period and was an essential element in Egyptian culture and religion. The ancient Egyptians believed that magic was an integral part of creation, and Heka was the force that enabled the gods to maintain order and balance in the world.

In Egyptian mythology, Heka played a significant role as the embodiment of magic and the power of divine forces. He was believed to be present during the act of creation, assisting the sun god Ra as he emerged from the primordial waters of Nun. Heka's power also extended to the daily lives of the Egyptians, as they believed that magic could be harnessed for both protective and destructive purposes.

Heka was associated with priests and healers, who were considered to have access to the magical powers necessary to heal ailments, protect individuals, or even manipulate the forces of nature. The practice of heka was considered both an art and a science, which required extensive knowledge of rituals, spells, and the properties of natural substances.

Throughout Egyptian history, Heka was revered as a symbol of the power of divine forces and the practice of magic. His connection to the natural world, the gods, and the act of creation made him an important figure in the religious and cultural life of ancient Egypt, embodying the belief that magic was an essential aspect of existence and the maintenance of order and balance in the world.

Serqet (or Selket)

Serqet, also spelled Serket or Selket, is a goddess in Egyptian mythology associated with protection, healing, and the power to counteract venom and poison. She is often depicted as a woman with a scorpion on her head or as a woman with the head of a scorpion, reflecting her close association with these venomous creatures.

The worship of Serqet dates back to the Old Kingdom and continued throughout Egyptian history. She was considered a powerful protector, not only against venomous bites and stings but also against various other dangers and misfortunes.

In Egyptian mythology, Serqet played a significant role as a protective and healing deity. She was believed to have the power to neutralize venom and poison, making her a vital figure in the treatment of snake bites, scorpion stings, and other venomous injuries. Serqet was also thought to protect the living from the various dangers and threats they faced, as well as safeguarding the deceased during their journey through the afterlife.

Serqet was one of the four goddesses (together with Isis, Nephthys, and Neith) who were believed to guard the four canopic jars used in the mummification process. These jars contained the internal organs of the deceased and were vital to their successful transition to the afterlife. Serqet's protective role in this context emphasized her importance in ensuring the well-being and eternal life of the deceased.

Throughout Egyptian history, Serqet was revered as a symbol of protection, healing, and the ability to counteract venom and poison. Her connection to the natural world, as well as her protective and healing powers, made her an important figure in the religious and cultural life of ancient Egypt, embodying the concepts of safety, preservation, and the triumph of life over death.

CHAPTER 2: OTHER CHARACTERS OF EGYPTIAN MYTHOLOGY

While many Egyptian myths primarily focus on gods and goddesses, there are other characters, such as mortals, demi-gods, heroes, prominent pharaohs, creatures, and monsters, that play important roles in these stories. In this chapter we will introduce you to these important characters.

Imhotep

Imhotep, in Egyptian history, is not a mythological figure but rather a real historical person who later became deified due to his extraordinary accomplishments. He lived during the Third Dynasty of Egypt, serving under the Pharaoh Djoser as an architect, physician, and vizier. Imhotep is best known for designing and constructing the Step Pyramid of Djoser at Saqqara, which is considered the earliest large-scale stone monument in Egypt.

Over time, Imhotep's reputation as an exceptional intellect and wise counselor grew, and he was eventually deified during the Late Period of ancient Egypt, around 2,000 years after his death. As a deity, Imhotep became associated with medicine, healing, and wisdom. He was often linked to the god Thoth, who was also revered for his wisdom and knowledge.

In his divine form, Imhotep was usually depicted as a seated man holding a papyrus scroll, signifying his status as a learned and wise individual. His cult was centered in Memphis and attracted devotees seeking wisdom, knowledge, and healing. The Greeks, who admired Egyptian culture and wisdom, identified Imhotep with their own god of medicine, Asclepius.

While Imhotep was not a mythological figure in the traditional sense, his extraordinary accomplishments in life and his eventual deification made him an important figure in the religious and cultural life of ancient Egypt. His association with medicine, wisdom, and architecture exemplified the ancient Egyptians' deep respect for knowledge and their reverence for individuals who contributed significantly to their civilization.

Menes (or Narmer)

Menes is another figure from Egyptian history, rather than mythology, who is traditionally credited with the unification of Upper and Lower Egypt. Menes is often identified as the first pharaoh of the First Dynasty, which marked the beginning of the Early Dynastic Period of ancient Egypt. However, his historical existence is still a subject of debate among scholars, and some suggest that Menes could be a legendary figure or a composite of several historical rulers.

The unification of Upper and Lower Egypt under Menes' rule is considered a pivotal event in Egyptian history, as it laid the foundation for a strong and centralized state. This unification was symbolically represented by the Pschent, a double crown combining the Red Crown of Lower Egypt and the White Crown of Upper Egypt.

Menes is also credited with founding the city of Memphis, which would become the capital of Egypt for much of its early history. Memphis was strategically located near the border of Upper and Lower Egypt, allowing the pharaoh to control and administer both regions effectively.

Although Menes is not a mythological figure, his role in the founding of the Egyptian state and the unification of Upper and Lower Egypt made him an important and legendary figure in Egyptian history. His legacy has been preserved in the form of numerous stories and legends that highlight his role as a pivotal ruler and the founder of the Egyptian civilization as it is known today.

Ra-Horakhty

Ra-Horakhty, also known as Ra-Harakhte, is a composite deity in Egyptian mythology, resulting from the fusion of the sun god Ra and the sky god Horus. This combination represented a synthesis of their attributes and symbolized the power of the sun and the sky.

In ancient Egyptian religion, Ra was the god of the sun and creation, while Horus was a sky god, often depicted as a falcon or a man with a falcon's head. The fusion of Ra and Horus into Ra-Horakhty emphasized the sun's path across the sky, with Horus' association with the sky further reinforcing this connection.

Ra-Horakhty is typically depicted as a falcon-headed man wearing a solar disk on his head, sometimes encircled by a cobra. He was revered as the supreme solar deity and was often associated with the rising sun, representing the sun's daily journey across the sky.

In Egyptian mythology, Ra-Horakhty played a significant role as a representation of the sun's power and the dominion of the sky. As the god of the sun and sky, Ra-Horakhty was associated with light, creation, and kingship, symbolizing the pharaoh's divine authority and his role as a mediator between the gods and the people.

Throughout Egyptian history, Ra-Horakhty was worshipped as a symbol of the sun's strength and the unification of Ra and Horus' divine aspects. His association with the sun and the sky made him an essential figure in the religious and cultural life of ancient Egypt, embodying the concepts of light, creation, and divine power.

Apis

Apis is a sacred bull in Egyptian mythology and religion, closely associated with the gods Ptah and Osiris. The worship of Apis dates back to the First Dynasty of Egypt, making it one of the oldest and most enduring religious practices in ancient Egyptian culture.

Apis was believed to be a manifestation of the god Ptah, the creator god of Memphis, and a symbol of his creative powers. The bull was also linked to Osiris, the god of the afterlife, and was believed to serve as an intermediary between the gods and the people. The fusion of Ptah and Osiris in the form of Apis represented the union of life, death, and rebirth, reflecting the ancient Egyptians' understanding of the natural cycles.

The Apis bull was chosen from the herds based on specific markings, such as a triangular white patch on its forehead and other distinctive patterns. Once selected, the bull was brought to the city of Memphis, where it was housed in a special temple complex known as the Serapeum. The bull was treated with great reverence, and its well-being was believed to ensure the fertility of the land and the prosperity of the people.

Upon its death, the Apis bull was mummified and buried with elaborate ceremonies in the Serapeum. The Egyptians believed that the soul of the deceased Apis bull would join Osiris in the afterlife and continue to serve as an intermediary between the gods and the people.

The worship of the Apis bull was an essential aspect of ancient Egyptian religion, reflecting the culture's deep reverence for animals and their connection to the divine. The Apis bull's association with the gods Ptah and Osiris symbolized the unity of life, death, and rebirth, making it a vital figure in the religious life of ancient Egypt.

Aker

Aker is a primordial earth deity in Egyptian mythology, often depicted as a double-headed lion or as two lions facing opposite directions. The name "Aker" means "bender" or "one who bends," which refers to the way the earth bends around the horizon. Aker represents the earth's surface and the horizon where the sun rises in the east and sets in the west.

Aker's role in Egyptian mythology is closely linked to the sun's journey through the underworld during the night. As the guardian of the gates of the eastern and western horizons, Aker was believed to protect the sun god Ra during his nightly voyage through the underworld, ensuring his safe passage and eventual rebirth at dawn. Aker was also considered a protector of the deceased, helping them during their journey through the underworld and ensuring their safe transition to the afterlife.

In some depictions, Aker is shown holding the akhet symbol, which represents the horizon and the concept of the sun rising and setting. This connection between Aker and the sun's cycle is a reflection of the ancient Egyptians' understanding of the natural world and their belief in the importance of the sun's daily journey for the renewal of life.

Aker's role in Egyptian mythology as the guardian of the eastern and western horizons emphasizes the significance of the sun's cycle and the balance between life, death, and rebirth. As a protector of both the sun god and the deceased, Aker symbolizes the interconnectedness of the natural world and the divine, reinforcing the ancient Egyptians' belief in the importance of harmony and balance in the universe.

Ammit

Ammit, also known as Ammut or "the Devourer," is a fearsome female demon in Egyptian mythology with a unique and terrifying appearance. She is often depicted as having the head of a crocodile, the body of a lion, and the hindquarters of a hippopotamus, representing the three largest man-eating animals known to the ancient Egyptians.

Ammit played a crucial role in the judgment of the dead in the afterlife. When a person died, their heart would be weighed against the feather of Ma'at, the goddess of truth, justice, and cosmic order, in a ceremony known as the Weighing of the Heart. If the heart was found to be heavier than the feather, it was considered impure and unworthy of entering the afterlife. At this point, Ammit would devour the impure heart, causing the individual to be denied entry into the afterlife and suffer a second death.

Ammit's role in Egyptian mythology was not that of a goddess but rather a demoness who represented the consequences of failing to live a just and balanced life. Her presence in the Weighing of the Heart ceremony served as a deterrent to wrongdoing and a reminder of the importance of maintaining Ma'at, or balance, in one's life.

Although Ammit was a fearsome figure, she was not considered evil. Instead, she was an essential part of the Egyptian concept of divine justice, ensuring that those who failed to live in accordance with Ma'at would face the consequences of their actions. Her role in the judgment of the dead highlights the ancient Egyptians' belief in the importance of living a balanced and just life, as well as the consequences of failing to do so.

Bennu

Bennu is a mythological bird in Egyptian mythology, often associated with creation, renewal, and the sun. The Bennu bird is considered the Egyptian precursor to the Greek Phoenix, symbolizing rebirth and regeneration. The name "Bennu" is believed to be derived from the ancient Egyptian word "weben," meaning "to rise" or "to shine."

In Egyptian mythology, the Bennu bird played a significant role in the creation story. It was believed to have come into existence from the heart of Osiris, the god of the afterlife, and to have flown over the primordial waters of Nun before landing on a sacred stone, known as the benben stone. The bird then let out a loud cry that broke the silence of the universe and marked the beginning of time.

The Bennu bird was closely associated with the sun god Ra and was considered his ba, or soul. The bird's connection with the sun made it a symbol of resurrection and renewal, as it was believed to be reborn with the rising sun each day. The Bennu was also associated with the cycle of time and the concept of eternity, as it was said to live for 500 years before creating a new Bennu from its own ashes.

In Egyptian art, the Bennu bird is often depicted as a large heron with a long beak and a two-feathered crest. It is sometimes shown perched atop the benben stone or a sacred obelisk, symbolizing its role in the creation story and its connection to the sun.

The Bennu bird's role in Egyptian mythology reflects the ancient Egyptians' understanding of the cycles of nature and their belief in the concept of rebirth and regeneration. As a symbol of creation, renewal, and the sun, the Bennu bird represents the interconnectedness of life, death, and the divine, emphasizing the importance of balance and harmony in the natural world.

The Ogdoad

The Ogdoad, also known as the Hermopolitan Ogdoad, refers to a group of eight primordial deities in Egyptian mythology, originating from the ancient city of Hermopolis. The Ogdoad is not a single deity but rather a collection of four male-female pairs, with each pair representing a fundamental aspect of the cosmos.

The four male gods of the Ogdoad are Nun, Amun, Kuk, and Huh, while their female counterparts are Naunet, Amaunet, Kauket, and Hauhet. The males are often depicted with frog heads, and the females with snake heads. These gods symbolize different aspects of the primordial chaos from which the world was created: Nun and Naunet represent the primordial waters, Amun and Amaunet signify hiddenness, Kuk and Kauket embody darkness, and Huh and Hauhet represent boundlessness or infinity.

In the creation myths associated with the Ogdoad, it is believed that these gods existed before the world was formed. They dwelled in the chaotic waters of Nun and eventually interacted to give rise to the first land, which emerged from the waters as a mound. Atop this mound, the sun god Ra was born, marking the beginning of creation and the world as known to the ancient Egyptians.

The Ogdoad's role in Egyptian mythology emphasizes the ancient Egyptians' understanding of the origins of the universe and their belief in the importance of balance and duality. By embodying the forces of chaos and order, the Ogdoad highlights the interconnectedness of the natural world and the divine, reinforcing the ancient Egyptians' belief in the necessity of harmony and balance in the cosmos.

The Sebau

In Egyptian mythology, the Sebau (or Sebau-fiends) are malevolent entities or spirits associated with chaos and disorder. They are considered the adversaries of the gods, particularly the sun god Ra, and were believed to create obstacles and difficulties for both the deities and the living. The Sebau-fiends are not a single entity, but rather a group of malevolent beings that work together to spread chaos and disrupt the cosmic order.

One of the most notable myths involving the Sebau-fiends is their attempt to impede the journey of Ra's solar barque through the underworld during the night. They sought to obstruct Ra's passage, trying to prevent the sun from rising again and plunging the world into eternal darkness. In this myth, the Sebau-fiends are defeated by the gods who accompany Ra, such as Set, who protects the solar barque from various threats during its nightly journey.

The Sebau-fiends are not typically depicted in Egyptian art, as they represent the forces of chaos that the Egyptians sought to avoid or overcome. However, their presence in the mythology serves as a reminder of the constant struggle between the forces of order and chaos in the cosmos.

The Seven Hathors

The Seven Hathors are a group of goddesses who are considered the manifestations of Hathor, the goddess of love, fertility, and motherhood. The Seven Hathors are associated with fate, destiny, and the protection of women and children.

The Seven Hathors are often depicted as cow-headed goddesses, reflecting the connection to Hathor, who is frequently portrayed with the head of a cow or wearing a headdress featuring cow horns and a solar disk. They are also sometimes shown as seven young women carrying musical instruments, such as tambourines or sistra, which are associated with Hathor's role as the goddess of music, joy, and celebration.

In Egyptian mythology, the Seven Hathors played a crucial role in determining the fate of newborn children. Upon the birth of a child, they would visit the family and declare the child's destiny by predicting important events in their life. This included aspects such as their profession, their future relationships, and even the manner of their death. The Seven Hathors were also believed to protect women during childbirth and ensure the safe delivery of babies.

Another aspect of the Seven Hathors' role in mythology is their presence at the Judgment of the Dead. They were thought to assist in weighing the heart of the deceased against the feather of Ma'at, thus participating in the determination of a person's afterlife fate.

The Seven Hathors serve as a reminder of the ancient Egyptians' belief in destiny and the idea that the course of one's life was predetermined by the gods. Their role in Egyptian mythology emphasizes the importance of fate, protection, and the nurturing aspects of the goddess Hathor, which were highly valued in Egyptian society.

Sphinx

The Sphinx is a mythical creature in Egyptian mythology, known for its unique appearance, which combines the body of a lion and the head of a human, often a pharaoh. Although the Sphinx is not a specific deity in Egyptian mythology, it represents a powerful symbol associated with protection, wisdom, and the strength of the pharaohs.

In ancient Egypt, sphinxes were frequently used as guardian statues, placed at the entrances to temples or tombs, to protect the sacred spaces from evil forces and intruders. The Great Sphinx of Giza, one of the most famous examples, is believed to be a depiction of the Pharaoh Khafre, who built the second-largest pyramid at Giza. The Great Sphinx represents the pharaoh's power, authority, and divine connection, as it stands guard over his burial complex.

Although the Sphinx is not a central figure in Egyptian myths, its association with protection and divine power has led to its incorporation into various legends and stories. One such story is the Greek myth of the Riddle of the Sphinx, which, although not originally Egyptian, has become closely connected with the image of the Sphinx. In this myth, the Sphinx poses a riddle to travelers, and if they fail to answer it correctly, the Sphinx kills them.

The Sphinx's role in Egyptian mythology and symbolism emphasizes the ancient Egyptians' beliefs in the protective power of their rulers and their connection to the divine. The Sphinx also serves as a lasting symbol of the grandeur and mystique of ancient Egyptian civilization.

Uraeus

Uraeus is not a deity in Egyptian mythology but rather a symbol of protection, power, and sovereignty. The term "uraeus" refers to the rearing cobra, specifically the Egyptian cobra, a venomous snake native to the region. This symbol is strongly associated with the Egyptian goddess Wadjet, who was the patron goddess of Lower Egypt and one of the earliest Egyptian deities.

In ancient Egyptian art, the uraeus is often depicted as a rearing cobra with its hood expanded, ready to strike. The uraeus was commonly used as a symbol of divine protection and was worn by pharaohs, particularly on their headdresses, as a symbol of their connection to the gods and their divine right to rule. This emblem is also frequently found on the crowns and diadems of various Egyptian deities, indicating their authority and protective aspects.

The uraeus is believed to have both protective and destructive powers. As a symbol of protection, it guarded the pharaohs, gods, and sacred spaces from enemies and evil forces. The uraeus was also thought to possess the ability to spit fire or venom at the enemies of the pharaoh or the gods, acting as a divine weapon.

The role of the uraeus in Egyptian mythology and symbolism underscores the importance of protection, divine authority, and the connection between the pharaohs and the gods. The uraeus serves as a potent symbol of the power and mystique of ancient Egyptian civilization and its religious beliefs.

Anpu

Anpu, also known as Anubis, is a character in the ancient Egyptian story called "The Tale of Two Brothers." In this tale, Anpu is the older brother of Bata. He is a farmer and married, while his younger brother Bata helps him with his work. Anpu's role in the story revolves around themes of loyalty, trust, and jealousy. When his wife falsely accuses Bata of attempting to seduce her, Anpu becomes enraged and seeks to kill his brother. However, Bata manages to convince him of his innocence. The tale follows the brothers' trials and tribulations, with Anpu eventually helping Bata regain his life and reunite with his wife. Although Anpu's character in this story is not the same as the god Anubis, the name similarity can sometimes cause confusion.

Bata

Bata is a central character in the ancient Egyptian myth known as "The Tale of Two Brothers." While not a god, Bata plays a significant role in this Egyptian narrative, which revolves around his relationship with his older brother, Anubis (not to be confused with the god of the afterlife). The tale is a story of love, betrayal, and redemption, showcasing themes of morality and divine intervention in ancient Egyptian culture.

The Griffin

The griffin is a mythical creature that has appeared in various mythologies, including ancient Egyptian mythology. It is typically depicted as a hybrid creature with the body of a lion and the head and wings of an eagle. Griffins in Egyptian myths are not central figures but rather hold symbolic roles and are often associated with the sun and divine power.

In Egyptian mythology, the griffin is linked to the sun god Ra and is believed to represent his power, strength, and protection. It was thought to guard treasures and sacred spaces, symbolizing the vigilance and guardianship required to protect valuable or divine possessions. Griffins can be found as decorative elements in Egyptian art, architecture, and jewelry, where they were used as symbols of authority, protection, and the divine.

The griffin's role in Egyptian mythology is not as prominent as it is in other mythologies, such as Greek and Persian, but it still holds significance as a symbol of divine power and protection.

Serpopards

Serpopards are mythical creatures that appear in ancient Egyptian and Mesopotamian art and mythology. They are depicted as hybrid creatures with the body of a leopard and the long, sinuous neck of a serpent. The name "serpopard" is a modern term that combines the words "serpent" and "leopard" to describe their appearance.

Although serpopards are not central figures in Egyptian mythology, they have been featured in various artistic representations, particularly during the Predynastic and Early Dynastic periods. Serpopards are often found on decorative items like the Narmer Palette, a ceremonial artifact dating back to around 3100 BCE, which marks the unification of Upper and Lower Egypt under the first pharaoh, Narmer.

The exact role and significance of serpopards in Egyptian mythology remain uncertain, as they are not mentioned in any specific myths or texts. However, they are believed to symbolize chaos and the untamed forces of nature. Their inclusion in royal and ceremonial art could represent the pharaoh's power to maintain order and control over these chaotic forces.

CHAPTER 3: CREATION MYTHS

There are many different creation myths in Egyptian Mythology, as different regions and time periods in ancient Egypt had their own unique versions of the creation story. However, there are several major creation myths that are widely known and studied today. In this chapter, we will cover four of the most prominent ones.

Hermopolis Myth

The Hermopolis creation myth, originating from the ancient Egyptian city of Hermopolis, is centered around the Ogdoad, a group of eight primordial deities that represented the elemental forces existing before the creation of the world. The myth emphasizes the concept of the cosmos emerging from a chaotic, formless state and the role of the Ogdoad in this process.

The Ogdoad consists of four male-female pairs of deities, representing different aspects of the primordial chaos:

1. Nun (male) and Naunet (female) – symbolizing the primordial waters or the watery abyss.

2. Kuk (male) and Kauket (female) – representing the darkness.

3. Huh (male) and Hauhet (female) – embodying the concept of infinity or boundlessness.

4. Amun (male) and Amaunet (female) – signifying hiddenness or that which is concealed.

In the beginning, there was only chaos and darkness, represented by the watery abyss of Nun. The Ogdoad resided within this chaotic expanse, and their existence personified the various aspects of the primordial state. They were depicted as beings with the heads of serpents and frogs, symbolizing their association with the water.

As time passed, the waters of Nun started to recede, revealing a mound of land known as the "Island of Flame" or the "Primeval Mound." According to some versions of the myth, a celestial goose, the "Great Cackler," laid an egg on this mound, which eventually hatched into the sun god, Ra. In other versions, the sun god, Atum, emerged from a lotus flower that bloomed on the mound or simply self-created himself on the spot.

Once the sun god came into existence, he began the process of creation, starting with the formation of the air god, Shu, and the moisture goddess, Tefnut. These two deities went on to create the earth god, Geb, and the sky goddess, Nut, who in turn gave birth to the divine siblings Osiris, Isis, Seth, and Nephthys.

As the cosmos continued to form, the Ogdoad deities receded in importance. Their essence became absorbed into the newly created gods, or they simply died off, symbolizing the transformation from chaos to order. The divine order, known as Ma'at, became a central concept in ancient Egyptian religion and philosophy, with the sun god, Ra, at its core.

In this way, the Hermopolis creation myth tells the story of how the chaotic, formless world was transformed into an ordered cosmos by the will of the sun god and the diminishing role of the primordial Ogdoad. The myth reflects the ancient

Egyptians' understanding of the universe's origins and their ongoing struggle to maintain order and balance in the face of chaos.

Heliopolis Myth

The Heliopolis creation myth, originating from the ancient Egyptian city of Heliopolis, is one of the most significant creation stories in Egyptian mythology. It focuses on the sun god, Atum, who is also associated with Ra, and the Ennead, a group of nine major deities that played essential roles in the creation process.

According to the Heliopolis creation myth, before the world existed, there was only the primordial waters of chaos, known as Nun. From these waters, a mound of land emerged, which is referred to as the "Primeval Mound" or the "Benben Stone." Atum, the sun god, either self-created himself on this mound or was born from the waters of Nun.

Atum, representing the essence of all things, was initially a singular being, embodying both male and female aspects. To begin the process of creation, Atum engaged in an act of self-procreation, producing the first divine couple: Shu, the god of air, and Tefnut, the goddess of moisture. In some versions of the myth, Atum produces Shu and Tefnut by either spitting them out or through an act of masturbation.

Shu and Tefnut left Atum to explore the watery chaos of Nun, and during their absence, Atum became worried and sent his Eye (also known as the "Udjat Eye" or "Eye of Ra") to search for them. Upon their return, Atum wept tears of joy, and it is said that from these tears, the first humans were born.

Shu and Tefnut went on to give birth to Geb, the god of the earth, and Nut, the goddess of the sky. The two were inseparable, locked together in a tight embrace. However, Shu, as the god of air, stepped in to separate them, lifting Nut above

Geb and creating the space between the earth and the sky. Nut was then filled with stars, becoming the celestial vault.

Geb and Nut produced four offspring: Osiris, Isis, Seth, and Nephthys. These divine siblings played essential roles in the mythology that followed, especially in the well-known story of Osiris, Isis, and Seth, which involves betrayal, resurrection, and the struggle for power.

The nine gods – Atum, Shu, Tefnut, Geb, Nut, Osiris, Isis, Seth, and Nephthys – form the Ennead of Heliopolis. The concept of Ma'at, or divine order, was central to the Heliopolitan myth, and it was the responsibility of the gods and the pharaohs to maintain this order in the face of chaos.

In summary, the Heliopolis creation myth tells the story of how the sun god Atum, born from the primordial waters of Nun, created the Ennead and the world as we know it. This myth not only explains the origins of the cosmos but also reflects the ancient Egyptians' understanding of the importance of maintaining balance and harmony in their world.

Memphis Myth

The Memphis creation myth, originating from the ancient Egyptian city of Memphis, is another significant creation story in Egyptian mythology. This myth revolves around the god Ptah, who was both the patron deity of Memphis and the god of craftsmen, and it highlights the power of thought and the spoken word in the process of creation.

According to the Memphis creation myth, before the world existed, there was only the primordial waters of chaos known as Nun. Ptah was the central figure in this creation story, and it was through his divine thoughts and creative utterances that the world came into being.

Ptah was seen as the master architect who envisioned the world and all of its components. His thoughts were the blueprints for creation, and it was through his heart (the seat of thought in ancient Egyptian belief) that the world's design was conceived. Once he had envisioned the world and all its elements, Ptah spoke the words that brought everything into existence.

The power of Ptah's spoken word was manifested through his tongue, which was associated with the god of wisdom and writing, Thoth. Thoth was believed to have been responsible for transcribing Ptah's creative thoughts into spoken and written language. As a result, Thoth played a crucial role in the process of creation, acting as the divine scribe who translated Ptah's thoughts into reality.

In the Memphis creation myth, all the other gods, including the members of the Ennead from the Heliopolis creation myth, were created by Ptah's thoughts and words. This notion placed Ptah in a superior position to the gods of Heliopolis, such as Atum and Ra. In this myth, the Ennead was seen as an extension of Ptah's creative power, rather than a separate group of deities responsible for creating the world.

The Memphis creation myth also emphasizes the importance of Ma'at, or divine order, just like the Heliopolis creation myth. Ptah was believed to have established the principles of Ma'at and to have ensured that the world operated according to these principles. As a result, the Memphis creation myth presents Ptah as the primary force responsible for maintaining balance and harmony in the world.

Thebes Myth

The Theban creation myth, originating in the ancient Egyptian city of Thebes (modern-day Luxor), is another important creation story in Egyptian mythology. This myth centers around the god Amun, who was the chief deity of Thebes and later became the preeminent god in the New Kingdom period. In this myth,

Amun is the central creative force, and it highlights his role as the self-created, hidden, and mysterious aspect of the divine.

According to the Theban creation myth, in the beginning, there was only the primordial waters of chaos, known as Nun. From this watery abyss, Amun emerged as a self-created deity. He was often depicted as a man wearing a crown with two tall plumes or as a ram-headed figure. The ram symbolized virility and creative power, and it was an important aspect of Amun's identity as the creator god.

Amun's name means "The Hidden One" or "The Invisible One," which reflects his enigmatic nature and role as the hidden force behind creation. He was believed to be the divine force that permeated all things and existed beyond human comprehension. In his hidden form, he was known as Amun-Kematef, which means "He who completes his moment," and Amun-Re, which simply means "the sun," highlighting his association with the sun god Ra.

In the Theban creation myth, Amun was responsible for creating all other gods and elements of the world. He did this by combining with his feminine counterpart, Amunet, who represented the hidden and mysterious aspect of the divine feminine. Together, they formed a creative dyad that gave birth to the world and all its components, including the gods of the Ennead.

The Theban creation myth also emphasizes the idea of Amun's continual self-renewal and regeneration. He was believed to create himself anew each day, symbolizing the eternal cycle of creation and regeneration. This concept is closely related to the daily cycle of the sun, which rises each morning, providing light and warmth to the world before setting and being reborn the following day.

The Theban creation myth presents Amun as the supreme deity, above all other gods, including those from the Heliopolitan and Memphite creation myths. This elevation of Amun to the position of the preeminent god was a political move by the Theban rulers to assert their religious authority over other regions of Egypt.

As a result, the Theban creation myth played a significant role in the consolidation of power during the New Kingdom period.

CHAPTER 4: LIFE IN ANCIENT EGYPT

Ancient Egypt was one of the most advanced and enduring civilizations of the ancient world, lasting for around 3,000 years from around 3100 BC to 332 BC. Life in ancient Egypt was centered around the Nile River, which provided fertile soil for agriculture, fresh water, and abundant resources such as fish and reeds. The Nile also served as a transportation system, connecting various cities and settlements throughout Egypt.

Social Structure

Ancient Egyptian society was hierarchical, with the pharaoh at the top, followed by the nobility, priests, government officials, soldiers, merchants, artisans, farmers, and slaves.

Pharaoh: The pharaoh was the supreme ruler of Egypt and was considered a living god. The pharaoh was responsible for maintaining Ma'at (cosmic order) and ensuring the prosperity and security of the nation.

Nobility: The nobility were the ruling class and included the royal family, high-ranking officials, and influential landowners. They had significant wealth and influence and often held key positions in the government and military.

Priests: The priesthood was responsible for conducting religious ceremonies, maintaining temples, and serving the gods. They held considerable influence in society due to their role in ensuring the gods' favor.

Government Officials: Government officials administered the daily affairs of the country, including tax collection, trade, agriculture, and public works projects.

Soldiers: The military class protected Egypt's borders, maintained internal security, and participated in foreign conquests.

Merchants and Traders: Merchants and traders were responsible for buying and selling goods, both domestically and internationally. They played a crucial role in the economy and contributed to Egypt's wealth.

Artisans: Artisans included skilled workers such as sculptors, painters, potters, weavers, and metalworkers. They created beautiful works of art and crafts, many of which were used in temples and tombs.

Farmers: The majority of the Egyptian population were farmers who cultivated the fertile land along the Nile River. They grew crops such as wheat, barley, flax, and various fruits and vegetables. The annual flooding of the Nile provided fresh silt that enriched the soil, making it ideal for agriculture.

Slaves: Slaves were at the bottom of the social hierarchy and were often prisoners of war or individuals who had fallen into debt. They performed various labor-intensive tasks, including working in the fields, quarries, and construction projects.

Religion and Worship

Religion was an integral part of daily life in ancient Egypt, and the people believed in a complex pantheon of gods and goddesses. These deities were believed to have control over the forces of nature and human affairs. Egyptians worshipped their gods through rituals, prayers, and offerings in order to maintain Ma'at and receive blessings.

Temples were the primary places of worship and were considered the homes of the gods. Each temple was dedicated to a specific deity and was maintained by priests who conducted daily rituals, such as offering food, clothing, and incense to the gods.

In addition to the state-sponsored religion, Egyptians also practiced household worship. They had small shrines in their homes, where they honored gods and goddesses, as well as their deceased ancestors. Personal piety and prayer were important aspects of daily life.

Festivals were also a significant part of religious life in ancient Egypt. Many festivals were held throughout the year to honor specific deities or celebrate significant events. One of the most famous was the Opet Festival, during which the statues of the gods Amun, Mut, and Khonsu were paraded from the Karnak temple to the Luxor temple.

Education and Writing

Education was an essential aspect of ancient Egyptian society, primarily reserved for the elite and the children of scribes. The Egyptian writing system, known as hieroglyphics, was used for religious texts, monumental inscriptions, and administrative records. Scribes were highly respected and well-educated individuals who played a vital role in the functioning of the government and religious institutions. They were responsible for recording laws, taxes, historical events, and religious texts.

Art and Architecture

Ancient Egyptians were skilled in various art forms and architectural feats. They built magnificent temples, palaces, and tombs that have endured the test of time. Egyptian art was characterized by a sense of order and balance, with strict rules governing proportions and perspective. Artists and craftsmen created sculptures, paintings, pottery, jewelry, and other decorative items that often depicted scenes from daily life, religious rituals, and myths.

Architecture in ancient Egypt was primarily focused on monumental structures, such as temples and tombs. The pyramids are the most famous examples of Egyptian architecture, built as tombs for pharaohs and their queens. The Great Pyramid of Giza, built for Pharaoh Khufu, is one of the Seven Wonders of the Ancient World and remains an impressive testament to the engineering and architectural prowess of the Egyptians.

Family Life and Gender Roles

Family was a central part of Egyptian society, and both men and women had specific roles within the family unit. The husband was typically the head of the household and responsible for providing for the family, while the wife was in charge of managing the home and raising the children. Women in ancient Egypt held a relatively high status compared to women in other ancient civilizations. They could own property, engage in business, and even hold positions of authority, such as priestesses and government officials.

Marriages were typically arranged, but they were based on mutual consent, and affection between spouses was considered important. Children were highly valued, and the Egyptians had a strong sense of love and responsibility towards their offspring.

In summary, life in ancient Egypt was deeply influenced by the Nile River, hierarchical social structure, and religious beliefs. This civilization produced great achievements in art, architecture, and education, as well as a rich cultural heritage that continues to captivate and inspire people to this day. Family life was central to Egyptian society, and both men and women had defined roles within their households, contributing to the stability and prosperity of the civilization.

CHAPTER 5: ISIS AND OSIRIS

The story of Isis and Osiris is one of the most famous and enduring myths from ancient Egyptian mythology. It revolves around themes of love, betrayal, resurrection, and the struggle for power. The myth highlights the relationship between Isis, the goddess of magic and healing, and Osiris, the god of the afterlife, as well as the roles of their siblings, Seth and Nephthys.

In the beginning, the gods Geb (the earth) and Nut (the sky) had four children: Osiris, Isis, Seth, and Nephthys. Osiris and Isis were married, as were Seth and Nephthys. Osiris was a wise and benevolent ruler of Egypt, teaching the people about agriculture, law, and civilization. His reign brought prosperity and order to the land.

However, Seth, the god of chaos and disorder, grew jealous of Osiris's success and popularity. Seth was known for his violence and destructive nature, and he resented his brother's peaceful rule. He devised a plan to usurp Osiris's throne and take control of Egypt.

Seth threw a lavish feast and invited Osiris and many other guests. During the festivities, he revealed a beautiful and ornate sarcophagus, claiming that he would gift it to the person who fit perfectly inside it. The guests took turns lying in the sarcophagus, but none of them fit perfectly. When it was Osiris's turn, he lay down inside, and the sarcophagus was a perfect fit. Seth immediately seized the opportunity, closed the lid, and sealed it with molten lead, trapping Osiris inside. He then threw the sarcophagus into the Nile River, which carried it to the shores of Byblos in modern-day Lebanon.

Isis, heartbroken by the loss of her husband, set out on a journey to find Osiris's body. She finally discovered it in Byblos, where a tamarisk tree had grown around the sarcophagus, encasing it within its trunk. The king of Byblos, unaware of what the tree contained, had used it as a pillar in his palace. Isis revealed her identity and persuaded the king to return the tree and the sarcophagus to her.

Isis brought the sarcophagus back to Egypt and hid it in the marshes of the Nile Delta to perform a ritual to resurrect Osiris. However, Seth discovered the body while out hunting and, in a fit of rage, dismembered it into 14 pieces, scattering them across Egypt. Undeterred, Isis embarked on another journey to recover Osiris's body parts. She found all but one piece—the phallus, which had been swallowed by a fish. Using her magical powers, she fashioned a new one from gold and reassembled Osiris's body.

With the help of Thoth, the god of wisdom and magic, and Anubis, the god of embalming and the dead, Isis performed a resurrection ritual. Osiris was brought back to life, but he could not remain among the living because he was incomplete. Instead, he became the ruler of the afterlife, the Duat, where he judged the souls of the deceased.

Isis, however, had conceived a son with the resurrected Osiris before he left for the afterlife. She gave birth to Horus, the falcon-headed god, and raised him in secret to protect him from Seth's wrath.

Isis understood that Horus's life would be in constant danger due to Seth's desire to eliminate any potential threat to his rule. To protect her son, Isis took Horus to a secluded place in the marshes of the Nile Delta, where they could remain hidden from Seth and his followers. Surrounded by the protective waters and vegetation, Isis raised Horus in secret, far from the prying eyes of her enemies.

During his childhood, Horus was educated and nurtured by his devoted mother. Isis taught him about his heritage, the legacy of his father Osiris, and the injustice that had befallen their family. As Horus grew older, he became increasingly aware of his destiny and the role he would play in avenging his father's murder and restoring order to Egypt.

Isis also ensured that Horus received divine guidance and protection. In some versions of the myth, other gods and goddesses, such as Thoth, the god of wisdom, and Hathor, the goddess of love and motherhood, assisted in Horus's upbringing. They provided him with the knowledge, skills, and wisdom he would need to fulfill his destiny and challenge Seth for the throne of Egypt.

As Horus reaches adulthood and becomes aware of his divine heritage and responsibility to avenge his father's death, he decides to confront Seth and claim the throne that rightfully belongs to him as the son of Osiris. This challenge ignites the long-standing rivalry between the two gods and marks the beginning of their epic struggle for power. To determine who should be the ruler of Egypt, Horus and Seth engage in a number of contests to prove themselves worthy.

The conflict between Horus and Seth is depicted as a series of battles, contests, and challenges that test their physical strength, cunning, and determination. These encounters are intense, reflecting the high stakes of their rivalry and the gods' powerful abilities.

One of the most famous episodes in the conflict involves a contest where each god is challenged to transform into a hippopotamus and remain submerged underwater for a set period. This competition is meant to test their strength and endurance, as well as their ability to control their divine powers. However, both gods eventually break the rules of the contest, resulting in a draw.

In the next competition, Horus and Seth engage in a boat race on the Nile, using boats made of stone. The race is meant to test their skill, speed, and control over the elements. Seth, in an attempt to gain an advantage, sabotages Horus's boat, but Horus cleverly outsmarts Seth by creating a boat made of wood and disguising it as stone. Ultimately, Horus emerges as the winner of the race, further angering Seth.

The conflict between Horus and Seth is also characterized by physical combat, with the gods engaging in fierce battles that cause destruction and chaos throughout Egypt. Their encounters are violent, and both gods suffer injuries during their confrontations. In one such battle, Seth gouges out one of Horus's eyes, while Horus retaliates by castrating Seth. The Eye of Horus, or Wadjet, later becomes a powerful symbol of protection and healing in Egyptian mythology.

The struggle between Horus and Seth is not only a battle between two powerful gods but also a symbolic representation of the struggle between order and chaos, good and evil, and the forces of life and death. As the god of the sky and rightful heir to the throne, Horus embodies the values of justice, order, and legitimate rule. In contrast, Seth represents chaos, violence, and disruption, as well as the forces of the desert and storms.

Throughout their conflict, the gods of Egypt are divided in their support for either Horus or Seth. Some align themselves with the rightful heir, Horus, while others are drawn to the powerful and unpredictable Seth. This division among the gods adds complexity to the struggle and further underscores the high stakes of the battle for Egypt's throne.

The gods, recognizing that the continuing struggle between Horus and Seth is causing great suffering and chaos throughout Egypt, convene a council to decide which of the two gods should rule the land. The council is composed of prominent gods and goddesses, including Ra, Thoth, Shu, and Tefnut, among others. Each god is called upon to share their opinion on who should be granted the throne, but the council finds itself divided still, with some gods siding with Horus and others supporting Seth.

The gods listen carefully to the arguments of both Horus and Seth. Horus emphasizes his divine right as the son of Osiris and rightful heir to the throne. He also points to Seth's treachery, including the murder of Osiris and the usurpation of the throne, as evidence that Seth is unfit to rule Egypt.

On the other hand, Seth argues that his strength and ability to maintain control over the land make him the most qualified candidate. He attempts to discredit Horus by highlighting his youth and inexperience, questioning his ability to protect Egypt and maintain order.

The gods, unable to reach a consensus, decide to seek the wisdom of Neith, a primordial goddess associated with wisdom, war, and creation. They ask her to provide guidance on which god should ascend to the throne. Neith considers the arguments of both Horus and Seth before advising the gods to award the throne to Horus, as he is the rightful heir and possesses the qualities needed to rule Egypt justly.

Neith also suggests that Seth be compensated for his loss by being given the hand of two goddesses, Anat and Astarte, in marriage. This proposal is an attempt to placate Seth and prevent further discord among the gods.

Following Neith's recommendation, the council of gods agrees to declare Horus the rightful ruler of Egypt. This decision marks the end of the long and destructive conflict between Horus and Seth and paves the way for a new era of peace and prosperity in the land.

After the council of gods declares Horus the rightful ruler of Egypt, Seth must face the consequences of his treachery and usurpation of the throne. Although he has been defeated, the gods do not entirely banish or destroy him, recognizing that he still holds an important role in the cosmic balance.

However, in some versions of the myth, Seth is banished to the desert, which is associated with his domain as the god of chaos, storms, and foreign lands.

This punishment is fitting, as it reflects his disruptive and destructive nature, and isolates him from the fertile, life-giving lands of Egypt.

In other accounts, Seth is given a crucial responsibility: to protect Ra, the sun god, during his nightly journey through the underworld. In this role, Seth battles the serpent Apep, also known as Apophis, a monstrous embodiment of chaos and darkness that seeks to devour Ra and plunge the world into eternal night. Despite his past actions, Seth's strength and ferocity prove invaluable in this role, as he courageously defends Ra from Apep's relentless attacks.

The story of Horus and Seth does not end with Seth's punishment; it also includes a moment of reconciliation between the two gods. While their rivalry and conflict are legendary, they eventually come to recognize their mutual interdependence and the need for balance between order and chaos. In some depictions, Horus and Seth join forces, combining their powers to create a harmonious and unified Egypt.

This reconciliation can be seen in the symbolic act of the two gods binding the plants of Upper and Lower Egypt, known as the "Sema Tawy" or the "Union of the Two Lands." This act signifies the restoration of harmony and the establishment of a united, prosperous kingdom under Horus's rule.

In some instances, Seth is even given a position of honor in the divine hierarchy, serving as a reminder that, despite his chaotic nature, he is still an essential part of the cosmic order.

The story of Isis, Osiris, Horus, and Seth had a significant impact on Egyptian religion and culture. The resurrection of Osiris symbolized the eternal cycle of death and rebirth, while the struggle between Horus and Seth embodied the ongoing conflict between order (Ma'at) and chaos (Isfet). The myth also served to legitimize the divine right of the pharaohs, who were considered to be the living incarnation of Horus and the rightful successors of Osiris.

In addition, the myth of Isis and Osiris contributed to the development of the concept of the afterlife in ancient Egypt. Osiris, as the ruler of the Duat, became a central figure in the funerary rites and beliefs of the Egyptians. The preservation and resurrection of Osiris's body served as the foundation for the practice of mummification, which was believed to ensure the soul's safe passage into the afterlife. The story of Isis and Osiris thus held deep cultural and religious significance, shaping the beliefs and practices of the ancient Egyptians for thousands of years.

CHAPTER 6: THE STORY OF RHODOPIS

The Girl with the Rose Red Slippers, also known as the Tale of Rhodopis, is an ancient Egyptian Cinderella-like story that has been dated back to the Greco-Roman period in Egypt, around 1st century BCE. The earliest written version is attributed to the Greek historian Strabo, who lived from 64 BCE to 24 CE.

Rhodopis was a beautiful and kind-hearted young girl who was a Greek slave in Egypt. She was treated poorly by her fellow slaves, who were jealous of her beauty and grace. They often mocked her and made her do all the hard work. However, Rhodopis remained cheerful and resilient despite the hardships she faced.

One day, as Rhodopis was bathing by the river, an eagle swooped down and snatched one of her rose-red slippers from the riverbank. The eagle carried the slipper all the way to the royal palace in Memphis, where Pharaoh Amasis was holding court.

The eagle dropped the slipper into the lap of Pharaoh Amasis, who was astonished by the beauty and the delicate craftsmanship of the slipper. Intrigued, he declared that he would search for the owner of the slipper and make her his queen, as he believed that a woman with such a beautiful slipper must be extraordinary.

Pharaoh Amasis ordered his servants to travel throughout the land to find the owner of the rose-red slipper. They searched far and wide until they finally reached the house where Rhodopis lived. She was brought before the Pharaoh, and when the slipper fit her perfectly, he knew that she was the one he had been searching for.

Pharaoh Amasis and Rhodopis were married in a grand ceremony, and Rhodopis became the queen of Egypt. Her life was transformed from a lowly slave to a beloved and respected queen, and she lived happily ever after with her king.

The story of the Girl with the Rose Red Slippers is one of the earliest recorded Cinderella-like tales and is believed to have inspired later versions of the story in various cultures around the world.

CHAPTER 7: THE TALE OF TWO BROTHERS

"Anpu and Bata" is an ancient Egyptian tale about two brothers, also known as "The Tale of Two Brothers." The story has been preserved in the Papyrus D'Orbiney, which dates back to the 19th Dynasty during the New Kingdom period. The narrative is divided into three parts, and it offers moral lessons and insights into ancient Egyptian society and religion.

Part 1: Anpu and Bata

Anpu and Bata are brothers, with Anpu being the elder of the two. Anpu is married and lives with his wife, while Bata, the younger brother, lives with them and helps with the daily work on the farm. The brothers share a strong bond, and Anpu trusts Bata completely. One day, while working in the field, Anpu sends Bata back to the house to fetch some seeds. Upon his arrival, Bata encounters Anpu's wife, who attempts to seduce him. Bata refuses her advances, citing his loyalty and respect for his brother.

Infuriated by the rejection, Anpu's wife concocts a false story, accusing Bata of attempting to seduce her. When Anpu returns home, his wife tearfully relays the fabricated account. Blinded by rage, Anpu plans to kill Bata.

Bata, however, is warned by divine intervention and flees. When Anpu catches up to him, Bata pleads his innocence and swears to his brother that he has been falsely accused. To prove his innocence, Bata severs his genitals and throws them into the water, where a fish swallows them. Convinced of his brother's innocence, Anpu mourns and regrets his actions.

Part 2: Bata and the Enchanted Tree

Bata, now castrated and unable to return to his previous life, seeks refuge in the Valley of the Cedar, where he builds a new home. The gods take pity on him and provide a beautiful wife, magically created from the essence of various divine beings.

Bata thrives in his new life, but he misses his brother Anpu. One day, he sends a message to Anpu via a pair of divine messengers, revealing his whereabouts and inviting him to visit. Anpu travels to the Valley of the Cedar and is amazed by Bata's new life. Bata informs Anpu that if he were to die, a beautiful flower would grow from the enchanted tree under which he now resides, and Anpu must retrieve the flower to bring him back to life.

In the meantime, Bata's beautiful wife betrays him by conspiring with a Pharaoh to take her away. Bata, heartbroken, dies of grief. As he had foretold, a flower blooms from the enchanted tree. A cow eats the flower, and, subsequently, the Pharaoh's new wife becomes pregnant, giving birth to a son who is, in fact, the reincarnation of Bata.

Part 3: Bata's Reincarnation and Reunion

Bata, now a prince, grows up in the Pharaoh's palace. He eventually becomes a general in the army and earns the Pharaoh's favor. Upon the Pharaoh's death, Bata inherits the throne and becomes the new Pharaoh.

During his reign, Bata seeks to reunite with his brother Anpu. He invites Anpu to the palace and reveals his true identity. Anpu is overjoyed to see his brother alive and well. Bata forgives Anpu for his past actions and offers him a high-ranking position in his court. The brothers live out the rest of their days in harmony, ruling the kingdom together.

The tale of Anpu and Bata emphasizes the importance of loyalty, trust, and the power of forgiveness. The story illustrates the bond between siblings, even when faced with deceit and betrayal. The narrative also explores themes of divine intervention, fate, and rebirth, as well as the consequences of one's actions.

In the context of ancient Egyptian society, the tale offers moral lessons and insights into the values that were important during that time. The strong bond between Anpu and Bata highlights the importance of family and loyalty, while the divine interventions throughout the story demonstrate the pervasive role of the gods in everyday life.

Furthermore, the tale showcases the concept of Ma'at, the ancient Egyptian principle of truth, balance, and justice, which was central to their belief system. Bata's vindication and rise to power reflect the triumph of truth and justice, while his eventual reunion and reconciliation with Anpu exemplify the importance of forgiveness and restoring balance to their relationship.

CHAPTER 8: THE JOURNEY OF RA

The journey of Ra, also known as the sun god, is a central theme in ancient Egyptian mythology. The Egyptians believed that Ra's daily journey across the sky and through the underworld (Duat) symbolized the cycle of life, death, and rebirth. The sun was seen as the source of life, and its journey represented the triumph of light over darkness and the forces of chaos.

Ra's journey can be divided into two main phases: his daytime journey across the sky and his nighttime journey through the underworld. Each phase had its unique challenges and encounters with various gods, goddesses, and creatures from Egyptian mythology.

The Daytime Journey:

Ra's daytime journey begins at dawn when he rises in the east as Khepri, the scarab god. In this form, Ra is depicted as a scarab beetle or a man with a scarab head, pushing the sun disc above the horizon. The scarab symbolizes rebirth and regeneration, as it lays its eggs in a ball of dung, which it rolls across the ground, mimicking the movement of the sun.

As the day progresses, Ra transforms into his midday form, taking on the appearance of a falcon-headed man with a solar disc on his head. In this form, he is often referred to as Ra-Horakhty, a combination of Ra and the sky god Horus. During his journey across the sky, Ra sails in a solar boat called Mandjet, accompanied by various gods and goddesses who help protect him from his enemies, most notably the chaos serpent Apep (Apophis).

The Nighttime Journey:

As the sun sets in the west, Ra takes on the form of Atum, the creator god, and descends into the underworld. In this phase, his solar boat is called Mesektet. Ra's journey through the Duat is fraught with dangers, as he must navigate through twelve regions or "hours," each with its own challenges and adversaries.

Throughout the night, Ra encounters various deities, spirits, and deceased souls. Some of the gods aid Ra in his journey, while others pose threats that he must overcome. One of the most significant challenges Ra faces is his nightly battle with Apep, a giant serpent representing chaos and destruction. Apep seeks to devour Ra and prevent the sun from rising again, which would plunge the world into eternal darkness.

Each night, Ra and his entourage engage in a fierce battle with Apep. The god Seth, who is often associated with chaos but also plays a protective role, is instrumental in helping Ra defeat the serpent. With Seth's assistance, Ra's boat and its divine occupants successfully fend off Apep, ensuring the sun's rebirth the following morning.

The journey of Ra through the underworld also serves as a model for the journey of the deceased in the afterlife. The dead were believed to follow Ra's path, overcoming various obstacles and facing judgment before Osiris, the god of the afterlife, to achieve eternal life.

In summary, the journey of Ra in Egyptian mythology represents the cycle of life, death, and rebirth. It emphasizes the importance of maintaining balance and order in the face of chaos, as well as the central role of the sun as the sustainer of life. The myth also provides a framework for understanding the afterlife, offering a symbolic map for the soul's journey to eternal life.

CHAPTER 9: THE BOOK OF THOTH

The story of the Book of Thoth is an ancient Egyptian myth about the power of knowledge, wisdom, and the consequences of accessing forbidden knowledge. The Book of Thoth, written by the god of wisdom and writing, Thoth, is said to contain the secrets of the universe, the knowledge of the gods, and the ability to understand the language of animals. The myth is preserved in a text known as the Papyrus of Setne Khaemwaset, dating back to the Ptolemaic Period (332-30 BCE).

The story revolves around the protagonist, Setne Khaemwaset, a prince, and son of Pharaoh Ramesses II. Setne is a learned and wise man, as well as a skilled magician. Despite his knowledge and abilities, Setne's desire for more power and wisdom leads him on a quest for the mythical Book of Thoth, which is said to grant extraordinary abilities to the person who reads it.

Setne learns about the Book of Thoth from an ancient scroll detailing the story of Nefrekeptah, a previous prince who found the book but suffered the tragic consequences of reading it. Nefrekeptah's body lies in a tomb at the bottom of the Nile, alongside the bodies of his wife, Ahwere, and their son, Merib. The Book of Thoth is sealed within the tomb, as a warning to those who would seek its power.

Ignoring the cautionary tale, Setne becomes determined to retrieve the book. He convinces his brother, Anherru, to join him on this dangerous mission.

Together, the brothers use their magical abilities to divine the location of the tomb. They perform rituals, call upon the gods for assistance, and cast spells that reveal the tomb's location at the bottom of the Nile. The brothers, determined to retrieve the book, journey to the site and use additional magic to descend to the depths of the Nile safely, where they find the entrance to the tomb.

Upon entering the tomb, Setne and Anherru discover that it is heavily guarded by various magical defenses, including serpents, scorpions, and fire. Undeterred, Setne uses his magical abilities to neutralize these threats, enabling the brothers to proceed further into the tomb.

As they reach the chamber where Nefrekeptah, Ahwere, and Merib's bodies lay, they find the Book of Thoth placed on a golden chest, bound with chains made of precious metals. At this moment, the ghost of Nefrekeptah appears, and in a solemn tone, he shares his own tragic story.

Nefrekeptah recounts how he, too, had sought the Book of Thoth, believing it would grant him unparalleled power and wisdom. He managed to find the book and learn its secrets, but the price he paid was devastating. As punishment for daring to access the forbidden knowledge, the gods took the lives of his beloved wife, Ahwere, and their son, Merib. Wracked with grief, Nefrekeptah ultimately decided to bury the book with his family, hoping to prevent others from suffering the same fate.

Despite Nefrekeptah's warnings, Setne's desire for the book remains unshaken. Nefrekeptah then challenges Setne to a series of magical contests, stating that if Setne can best him, he may take the book. Setne accepts the challenge, and the two engage in a series of three trials, each showcasing their magical prowess.

1. *The Game of Senet:*

The first contest involves a game of Senet, an ancient Egyptian board game. Nefrekeptah tells Setne that he must defeat him in the game to proceed. However, the game is not an ordinary one – the pieces are enchanted and have a will of their own. Setne is initially intimidated, but his determination to possess the Book of Thoth enables him to focus and play skillfully. After a hard-fought match, Setne manages to outmaneuver Nefrekeptah and wins the game.

2. The Test of Riddles:

The second contest is a test of wisdom and intellect. Nefrekeptah poses a series of riddles for Setne to solve. These riddles are designed to be complex and challenging, testing Setne's knowledge and understanding of ancient Egyptian history, culture, and mythology. Setne carefully considers each riddle, drawing on his extensive knowledge as a high priest. Ultimately, he succeeds in answering each riddle correctly, demonstrating his intellectual prowess.

3. The Trial of Strength:

In the final contest, Nefrekeptah challenges Setne to a test of physical strength and endurance. Despite Setne's magical abilities, he is not known for his physical prowess. However, he understands that to obtain the Book of Thoth, he must prove his worth in this final trial. Setne and Nefrekeptah engage in a series of physical challenges, such as wrestling, weightlifting, and long-distance running. Through sheer determination and willpower, Setne manages to hold his own against Nefrekeptah's ghost and ultimately prevails.

Having successfully passed all three contests, Setne is deemed worthy by Nefrekeptah to possess the Book of Thoth. However, Nefrekeptah warns Setne that he will face severe consequences for his actions, as the book's power comes with a heavy price.

Setne, feeling triumphant, disregards Nefrekeptah's warning and takes the Book of Thoth. As the prince delves deeper into the secrets of the book, he inadvertently sets off a series of tragic events, leading him down a path of suffering and despair. Following his acquisition of the book of Thoth, the following events occur in Setne's life:

1. *Encounter with Taboubu:*

After acquiring the Book of Thoth, Setne comes across a beautiful woman named Taboubu. She is, in fact, a magical illusion created by Nefrekeptah to bring about Setne's downfall. Completely enamored by her beauty, Setne becomes infatuated with Taboubu and is willing to do anything to win her affection.

2. Disregard for family and morality:

Taboubu demands that Setne divorce his wife and send his children away to win her love. Blinded by desire, Setne agrees to her terms without hesitation, disregarding his family and moral values. This causes him to lose the love and respect of his family, as well as his own sense of morality.

3. Public humiliation:

Taboubu insists that Setne must sign a legal document agreeing to her terms, and she invites a large gathering of nobles and scribes to witness the event. Setne, still captivated by Taboubu, signs the document in front of the crowd, further tarnishing his reputation.

4. Taboubu's revelation:

After Setne signs the document, Taboubu reveals her true identity as an illusion sent by Nefrekeptah. She explains that her purpose was to teach Setne a lesson about the consequences of his greed and lust for power. The revelation leaves Setne humiliated and devastated, as his actions have caused irreparable damage to his life and reputation.

5. Loss of status and power:

As a result of his actions, Setne loses his prestigious position as a high priest and son of Pharaoh Ramesses II. His impulsive behavior and immoral actions, driven by his obsession with the Book of Thoth and Taboubu, have severe consequences on his life and standing in society.

Horrified by the consequences of his actions and the curse of the Book of Thoth, Setne returns to Nefrekeptah's tomb, seeking redemption. He pleads with Nefrekeptah to take back the book and help him right his wrongs. Nefrekeptah agrees, and Setne's life is restored to normalcy. Setne learns the hard way that some knowledge is best left undiscovered, and he gains a newfound respect for the wisdom of the gods.

The story of the Book of Thoth serves as a cautionary tale, warning of the dangers of seeking forbidden knowledge and the consequences of hubris. It also highlights the importance of respecting the boundaries set by the gods and understanding the limits of human wisdom and power. The myth underscores the belief that some knowledge should remain exclusive to the gods, and attempting to attain it can result in severe consequences for mortals.

CHAPTER 10: ISIS AND THE SEVEN SCORPIONS

In ancient Egyptian mythology, the story of Isis and the Seven Scorpions is a tale of devotion, cunning, and the power of a mother's love. It takes place during the tumultuous period following the murder of Isis' husband, Osiris, by his jealous brother, Seth.

After Osiris' death, Isis embarks on a perilous journey to recover her husband's dismembered body and restore him to life. Simultaneously, she seeks to protect her unborn son, Horus, from Seth's wrath, as the child is prophesized to avenge his father's death and take the throne. To aid her in this difficult quest, she is accompanied by seven loyal scorpions, each with unique powers and abilities.

To escape Seth's pursuit and find a safe haven to give birth to Horus, Isis must travel to the marshes of the Nile Delta, where she hopes to find sanctuary among the reeds. The seven scorpions, sensing the danger and the importance of their mission, form a protective entourage around the pregnant goddess. The scorpions are Tefen and Befen, the vanguards; Mestet and Mestetef, the scouts; and Petet, Thetet, and Maatet, who guard Isis directly.

As they journey through the desert, the scorpions merge their venom, creating a single, powerful dose. They entrust this potent venom to Petet, the leader of the group, who carries it in his stinger, ready to unleash it upon any threat they may encounter.

Weary from her journey, Isis arrives at a small village on the outskirts of the marshes, seeking shelter for the night. She approaches the home of a wealthy noblewoman, hoping to find a safe place to rest. However, the noblewoman, fearful of the scorpions and unaware of the goddess's true identity, callously turns Isis away.

Rejected and exhausted, Isis finds refuge in the humble dwelling of a peasant woman named Uatchet, who offers her a simple but warm shelter. Touched by Uatchet's kindness and generosity, Isis gratefully accepts her hospitality.

Angered by the noblewoman's cruel treatment of their mistress, the scorpions decide to exact vengeance. Under the cover of darkness, Tefen sneaks into the noblewoman's home and places the venomous stinger of Petet into the sleeping woman's child.

As the venom courses through the child's veins, the house is filled with the child's anguished cries. The noblewoman, desperate to save her son, seeks help from her neighbors, but none can offer a cure for the terrible poison afflicting the boy.

Hearing the child's cries, Isis recognizes the handiwork of her scorpion companions. Despite the noblewoman's earlier unkindness, Isis is moved by the mother's love for her child and her desperation. The goddess, in her infinite compassion, decides to intervene.

Isis enters the noblewoman's house and, with her divine powers, draws the venom from the child's body, saving his life. The noblewoman, now aware of Isis' true identity, falls to her knees in gratitude and begs for forgiveness. Isis, benevolent and wise, forgives the woman and imparts a valuable lesson about the importance of kindness and empathy.

In the end, Isis and her scorpion companions continue their journey, eventually reaching the safety of the marshes. There, in the seclusion of the reeds, Isis gives birth to Horus, the future king who will restore order to Egypt and avenge his father's death.

The story of Isis and the Seven Scorpions is a captivating tale that highlights the importance of empathy, compassion, and the power of a mother's love. It teaches us valuable lessons about offering kindness to strangers, as one never knows when they might be in the presence of a deity or someone in need.

The tale also illustrates the protective nature of Isis, who not only looks after her unborn son but also extends her compassion to a child who is not her own. It demonstrates the goddess's wisdom and her ability to see beyond the misdeeds of others, offering forgiveness and understanding.

CHAPTER II: THE DESTRUCTION OF MANKIND

In ancient Egyptian mythology, the story of the Destruction of Mankind is a compelling tale of divine wrath, cunning, and ultimately, redemption. It centers around the sun god Ra, who grows weary of humanity's insolence and decides to unleash his vengeance upon the world.

The story begins with Ra, the supreme god and ruler of the Egyptian pantheon, growing increasingly discontent with the actions of humanity. The people have become rebellious, disrespectful, and ungrateful, neglecting their duty to worship and honor the gods. In his anger, Ra decides that mankind must be punished for their insolence.

Ra summons a council of the gods to discuss the fate of humanity. During the deliberations, the council of gods contemplates the severity of humanity's actions and weighs the options available to punish them. At the same time, the council must also consider the impact of their decision on the future of mankind, as well as the potential consequences on the world they govern.

As the deliberations continue, the gods reach a consensus that humanity must face divine retribution for their disrespect and negligence. It is then proposed that the goddess Hathor, known for her dual nature as both a nurturing mother figure and a fierce warrior, should be the instrument of their wrath. In her terrifying form as Sekhmet, the lioness-headed goddess of war, Hathor would be the perfect embodiment of divine vengeance.

Ra, as the leader of the council and the supreme god, approves this plan and entrusts Hathor with the responsibility of punishing humanity. The council's decision sets the stage for the unfolding events in the story, as Hathor transforms into Sekhmet and unleashes her fury upon the world.

Sekhmet descends upon the earth and begins her bloody rampage, slaughtering countless humans in her path.

Sekhmet's rampage is a fearsome and bloody affair, as she sets out to unleash her divine fury upon humanity. She becomes the embodiment of divine wrath, mercilessly slaughtering those who have incurred the gods' displeasure through their disobedience and disrespect. As she moves through the land, her fierce gaze and razor-sharp claws bring death and chaos.

The earth is soaked with the blood of her victims, and the air is filled with the cries of those who cannot escape her wrath. Villages and cities are left in ruins, as the once-proud bastions of human civilization are reduced to smoldering rubble under the might of the vengeful goddess.

As Sekhmet's rampage continues, the surviving humans flee in terror, desperately seeking refuge from her relentless pursuit. They scatter across the land, hiding in remote corners of the world, hoping to escape the goddess's notice. The devastation left behind by Sekhmet is a stark reminder of the power of the gods and the consequences of defying their will.

Despite her initial resolve to carry out the divine punishment, Sekhmet's rampage eventually becomes a source of concern for Ra and the other gods. The sheer scale of the destruction and the indiscriminate nature of her wrath threaten to annihilate mankind entirely, disrupting the cosmic balance that the gods seek to maintain.

Recognizing that Sekhmet's unrelenting fury threatens the cosmic balance and the existence of mankind, Ra decides to intervene. His plan involves exploiting the goddess's warrior instincts and her current bloodlust to trick her into stopping her rampage.

To execute his plan, Ra orders his followers to brew a vast quantity of beer. This beer is then mixed with red ochre, a pigment with a deep red hue that resembles the color of blood. The idea behind this concoction is to create a beverage that appears like the blood of Sekhmet's victims, which would appeal to her bloodthirsty nature.

Once the beer and red ochre mixture is ready, Ra instructs his followers to pour it into the Nile, turning the river into a blood-red sea. As Sekhmet returns from her slaughter, she encounters the transformed Nile and, believing it to be filled with the blood of the humans she has slain, eagerly drinks from it.

The goddess, however, is unaware that she is consuming a potent beer, not blood. As she drinks more and more of the intoxicating mixture, she eventually succumbs to its effects. Sekhmet becomes drowsy and disoriented, her senses dulled, and her bloodlust diminished. In this weakened state, she is unable to continue her rampage and ultimately falls into a deep slumber.

Sekhmet, intoxicated and subdued by the beer and red ochre mixture, undergoes a transformation as her destructive fury subsides. While she sleeps, her wrathful form as the lioness-headed goddess of war and destruction recedes, and she reverts to her gentler form as Hathor, the goddess of love, joy, and motherhood.

When Hathor awakens from her slumber, she is no longer filled with the bloodlust and rage that had driven her rampage. Instead, the goddess is overcome with remorse for her actions and compassion for the surviving humans. As a deity who is typically associated with nurturing and love, this change of heart is fitting with her true nature. It reflects her dual nature as a fierce warrior and a loving protector, showcasing the complex and multifaceted aspects of the gods in Egyptian mythology.

With Hathor's fury quelled, humanity is granted a second chance. The remaining people, who had sought refuge from Sekhmet's wrath, can now emerge from their hiding places and begin to rebuild their lives. This act of mercy serves as a reminder of the importance of honoring the gods and adhering to the divine order, as well as the consequences of straying from this path.

CHAPTER 12: CATS AND BASTET

In ancient Egypt, cats were highly regarded for their grace, agility, and mysterious nature. They were considered sacred animals and were closely associated with the goddess Bastet (also known as Bast). Bastet, a protective goddess, was often depicted with the head of a lioness or as a domesticated cat. As the daughter of Ra, the sun god, she played an important role in Egyptian religion and culture.

Bastet was primarily a goddess of protection, love, fertility, and motherhood. She was the protector of the home, women, and children, and was believed to defend against evil spirits and diseases. Over time, her ferocious lioness features became gentler, and she was increasingly associated with domesticated cats, which were believed to possess protective qualities themselves.

Cats in ancient Egyptian society held a unique and important role. They were highly valued for their ability to hunt and kill vermin, such as mice and rats, which posed a threat to grain stores. Due to their natural hunting abilities, Egyptians saw cats as symbols of protection, and they became closely associated with Bastet.

The worship of Bastet took place primarily in the city of Bubastis, which was located in the Nile Delta. Bubastis became a major center for the cult of Bastet, attracting worshippers from across Egypt. During annual festivals dedicated to the goddess, thousands of devotees would visit the city to participate in processions, feasts, and celebrations in her honor. These festivities were often marked by music, dancing, and a general atmosphere of joy and revelry.

Cats were considered so sacred in ancient Egypt that many families kept them as pets and believed that having a cat in the home would invoke Bastet's protection. When a cat died, the family would often go into mourning and have the cat mummified, just as they would for human family members. The mummified remains of cats have been discovered in large quantities throughout Egypt, demonstrating the high regard in which they were held.

The story of cats and Bastet in Egyptian mythology reflects the importance of animals in the religious and cultural life of ancient Egypt. The reverence for cats and their association with the protective goddess Bastet exemplifies the complex relationship between humans and animals in Egyptian society, as well as the deep respect and admiration for the natural world that characterized ancient Egyptian culture.

CHAPTER 13: THE PRINCE AND THE SPHINX

The story of the Prince and the Sphinx is not a traditional Egyptian myth but rather a tale derived from various sources and influenced by different cultures, including Greek and Roman. This tale is a blend of the famous Greek myth of Oedipus and the Sphinx and the Egyptian concept of the Sphinx as a guardian figure.

In this story, a young Egyptian prince goes on a quest to save his city from the wrath of a malevolent Sphinx. The Sphinx is a mythical creature with the body of a lion and the head of a human, often associated with wisdom and riddles.

The tale begins when the Sphinx arrives at a city in Egypt and starts to terrorize its inhabitants. The creature poses a riddle to the people and declares that if they can solve it, he will leave them in peace. However, if they cannot find the answer, the Sphinx threatens to destroy the city and devour its people.

The terrified citizens desperately search for a solution, but none can unravel the Sphinx's enigmatic riddle. As despair grips the city, the young prince decides to take on the challenge himself, determined to save his people from the Sphinx's wrath.

Armed with courage and intelligence, the prince approaches the Sphinx and asks to hear the riddle. The Sphinx, confident that no one can solve its puzzle, poses the question: "What creature has one voice and yet becomes four-footed, two-footed, and three-footed?"

The prince ponders the riddle carefully, searching for an answer that will save his city. Finally, he realizes the solution and confidently responds: "The answer is a human. A human crawls on all fours as a baby, walks on two feet as an adult, and uses a walking stick as a third foot in old age."

Upon hearing the prince's answer, the Sphinx is taken aback, realizing that its riddle has been solved. True to its word, the creature ceases its rampage and leaves the city, freeing the people from its tyranny. The grateful citizens hail the prince as a hero, and he is celebrated for his wisdom and bravery.

While this tale is not a traditional Egyptian myth, it showcases the Sphinx as a symbol of wisdom and mystery in ancient Egyptian culture. The story also emphasizes the power of intellect and courage, qualities that were highly valued in ancient Egypt.

CONCLUSION

As our journey through "Egyptian Mythology: A Timeless Collection of Egyptian Myths and Legends" draws to a close, we find ourselves standing at the threshold between the ancient world and our own, forever changed by the stories of gods, heroes, and the people of ancient Egypt. We have traversed the sands of time, exploring the depths of creation myths, the intricacies of daily life in the Nile Valley, and the enduring tales of deities and mortals that have shaped the cultural legacy of one of humanity's earliest civilizations.

Through the chapters of this book, we have witnessed the timeless nature of Egyptian mythology, a testament to the human spirit's quest for understanding, meaning, and connection to the divine. The myths and legends recounted here are more than mere stories; they are the collective memory of a people, an intricate weave of cultural identity, spiritual beliefs, and cosmic understanding that has survived the erosion of time.

The tales of Isis and Osiris, the journey of Ra, and the wisdom of Imhotep, among others, are not just remnants of the past; they are living narratives that continue to inspire, intrigue, and inform our modern world. They remind us of the power of myth to transcend boundaries, to connect us across millennia to our ancestors, and to echo the universal themes of love, loss, redemption, and the eternal cycle of life and death.

Thank you for joining me on this journey. May these stories continue to inspire and enlighten, just as they have for generations past and, undoubtedly, for many generations to come.

I truly hope you have enjoyed this book. If you would like to share your feedback, it is greatly appreciated if you could take a moment to leave me a review on Amazon. It only takes around 1-minute, and it really helps me to continue producing books that readers love!

And finally, please keep an eye out for the other books in this series, also available for sale on Amazon as well as through many other online retailers. All current and upcoming books in this series are listed on the following page.

MORE BOOKS BY ADRIAN DANVERS

Did you enjoy this book on Egyptian Mythology?

If so, then keep an eye out for the 17 other books in this series, each dedicated to exploring the mythology from different ancient cultures! Depending upon the time of reading, not all of these titles will be available yet, but rest assured, they will be published very soon! These books are all available through Amazon, along with many other online retailers.

Other Books in this Series

Roman Mythology: A Timeless Collection of Roman Myths and Legends

Norse Mythology: A Timeless Collection of Norse Myths and Legends

Celtic Mythology: A Timeless Collection of Celtic Myths and Legends

Greek Mythology: A Timeless Collection of Greek Myths and Legends

Australian Aboriginal Mythology: A Timeless Collection of Australian Aboriginal Myths and Legends

Native American Mythology: A Timeless Collection of Native American Myths and Legends

African Mythology: A Timeless Collection of African Myths and Legends

Maya Mythology: A Timeless Collection of Maya Myths and Legends

Aztec Mythology: A Timeless Collection of Aztec Myths and Legends

Inca Mythology: A Timeless Collection of Inca Myths and Legends

Hindu Mythology: A Timeless Collection of Hindu Myths and Legends

Chinese Mythology: A Timeless Collection of Chinese Myths and Legends

Sumerian Mythology: A Timeless Collection of Sumerian Myths and Legends

Japanese Mythology: A Timeless Collection of Japanese Myths and Legends

Māori Mythology: A Timeless Collection of Māori Myths and Legends

Hawaiian Mythology: A Timeless Collection of Hawaiian Myths and Legends

Persian Mythology: A Timeless Collection of Persian Myths and Legends

For any questions about upcoming books, or feedback you'd like to share, please reach out to adrian@adriandanvers.com

Printed in Great Britain
by Amazon